The True Church and Morality

Duncan
Forrester

The True Church and Morality

Reflections on Ecclesiology and Ethics

Risk
BOOK SERIES

WCC Publications, Geneva

1-20-98

Cover design: Edwin Hassink

ISBN 2-8254-1193-0

© 1997 WCC Publications, World Council of Churches,
150 route de Ferney, 1211 Geneva 2, Switzerland

No. 74 in the Risk Book Series

Printed in Switzerland

Table of Contents

Preface

This is a book of reflections arising out of the World Council of Churches' Ecclesiology and Ethics study project, in which I was involved. The study was established for various reasons. For many years there has been an uncertain relationship and sometimes tension between the ecumenical movement's concerns with doctrine and unity on the one hand and with social witness and action for peace and justice on the other. Sometimes the social activists speak of doctrinal dialogues as irrelevant to the real needs of the world, while the theologians regard the activists as side-stepping the most difficult and enduring issues in order to respond to the needs of the moment.

In recent times the recognition has grown that the being and mission of the church can be at stake when it wrestles with hard ethical choices. We need to reconsider how ethics and doctrine are intertwined, and realize that they cannot be easily separated out. In struggles for liberation and justice many have found an experience of solidarity, unity and fellowship so profound that it has sometimes been spoken of as constituting a new understanding of what it is to be church. In some cases the same causes that have brought people together in a unity of struggle have also caused divisions in the church, as in the German church struggle in the 1930s or the more recent struggle against apartheid in South Africa — divisions which in some ways may have been necessary, and have pointed the way to a more genuine fellowship or *koinonia*.

I hope this book will encourage readers to become involved in this debate, which is far from concluded and which is of the greatest importance for the integrity of the church in its search for unity and faithful discipleship.

I am particularly grateful for much stimulus and help in my thinking on these matters to all those who took part in the WCC consultations on ecclesiology and ethics at Jerusalem in 1994 and at Johannesburg in 1996, and to staff of the WCC, particularly Tom Best, Martin Robra and Alan Falconer.

Perhaps I can use as a kind of motto for this book some words of my friend, the ecumenical veteran Ian Fraser:

> I have argued all along... that there is no subject or discipline which can be labelled "ethics"; there is just the vivid interplay between theology (as the faith-basis for changing history towards the kingdom) and concrete reality which should issue in imaginative communal obedience. Ethical behaviour is a struggle for the church to be the church.

I don't think that the theme of this book could be put more incisively.

Edinburgh   DUNCAN B. FORRESTER
All Saints' Day, 1996

1. Church and Ethics Yesterday and Today

It is a commonplace to say that the Christian faith and the Christian church are concerned with morality. All over the world the church is expected to pronounce on moral issues, although many would want to limit its remit to personal morality and denounce it when it strays beyond into making pronouncements on political and economic matters, regarding these as technical and beyond its competence. So it is welcomed when it supports traditional "family values", criticized when it speaks on economic and political matters, when it opposes oppression, when it speaks for the poor and exploited. On some moral issues there are deep divisions between Christian traditions and within churches; attitudes to homosexuality, contraception or abortion are good examples. On other issues, such as the evil of apartheid and racism, there is a growing consensus among Christians and churches. The modern ecumenical movement has led to some significant convergences among the churches on ethical matters; but it has also highlighted the depth and gravity of other ethical differences. Sometimes shared ethical concerns draw Christians into a fuller sense of community. But ethical disagreements can be bitterly divisive.

In the past it was often assumed that it was almost impossible to be moral unless one had faith. Hardly anyone believes that nowadays, but the church is still regarded by many as an important agency of moral education and nurture, a powerful reinforcement to ethical behaviour, a kind of moral glue holding society together. Indeed, people frequently assume that Christianity is about morality and nothing more. Faith then becomes a set of imaginative sanctions against wrongdoing, a way of encouraging goodness. On this view, the church is seen as a pillar of the traditional, accepted morality, whose central task is conserving, defending, commending a moral tradition and inculcating a received moral wisdom.

In a sense all this is right and proper. The Christian faith *is* concerned with morality and with goodness, although in a far more complex and disturbing way than many people assume.

Ethics and unity in the Bible

In the Bible moral and doctrinal teaching are interwoven in a subtle and significant manner, suggesting that you cannot have one without the other. The indicative and the imperative are inseparably bound together. The command is rooted in the story. The ten commandments are presented as given by the living God who proclaims, "I am the Lord your God, who brought you out of the land of Egypt, out of the house of slavery" (Ex. 20:2). Their authority for Israel arises from the fact that the people have been delivered by the God who has bound himself to them in covenant-love. In their dealings with this God the people hear God's command and discover what they ought to do. Because they have experienced the bitterness of slavery and the contempt often visited upon strangers and outsiders, and because they have encountered a God who cares passionately for the forgotten and hears the cry of the poor, they are to be hospitable and gentle towards the strangers in their midst, and open-handed towards the poor.

In the New Testament, too, doctrine, story and moral teaching are woven together into a seamless web. In the epistles, ethics is not a mere postscript to doctrinal teaching but an inseparable part of what it is to be a believer. And in the gospels it is abundantly clear that being a disciple, following Jesus, involves a life-style, a discipline, a strenuous way, a wrestling with moral choices. Indeed, in and through the moral life we come to know God: "those who do what is true come to the light, so that it may be clearly seen that their deeds have been done in God" (John 3:21). And the First Letter of John declares that "everyone who loves is born of God and knows God. Whoever does not love does not know God, for God is love" (1 John 4:7-8). Being a disciple, confessing the faith, involves a particular loving stance on life and on action.

But Christianity is not legalistic. The life-style for Christians is not cast in bronze, immutable and hard. Because they believe that the source of all good is the *living* God, Christians have to learn to attend to God's call and to rely on God's grace

— and on God's forgiveness when they go astray. And since ethics is essentially a relationship to God, believers struggle to discern the signs of the times, to understand what God is doing and calling on his people to do.

Nor is Christian morality individualistic. We act and exist in solidarity with others, with a vast company of people bound to us by ties of mutual responsibility and accountability. Believers see themselves as part of the Body, working in harmony with the Body, sustained by the Body. The Body is the steward of disturbing memories and hopes which put the present into a new perspective. In the Body the various members depend upon one another, support one another and forgive one another. They have different functions, tasks, callings and responsibilities, but within the Body the ranking and hierarchy of society is transcended or reversed. All are necessary; each is of infinite worth and dignity. And in the Body the conflicts and animosities and divisions of society are overcome in shared concern for one another, in mutual honouring. In the words of one of the classic New Testament passages about the Body, "if one member suffers, all suffer together with it; if one member is honoured, all rejoice together with it" (1 Cor. 12:26).

The existence of the Body is in itself a moral statement, a demonstration and exemplification of the ethic which is integral to the gospel. The behaviour of the community confirms or questions the truth of the gospel which its members proclaim. Lesslie Newbigin brings this out with a story of preaching in a South Indian village. The preacher stands in the open air, with the little Christian congregation gathered around to listen. But others are listening too — from a distance, through open windows, from the shade of a great banyan tree, even with backs turned on the preacher. The villagers who are not Christians *hear* the preacher's words. But they also *see*, in front of them, their Christian neighbours. And if they know that these neighbours' lives are immoral or that the little village congregation is riven with animosities and hostility, it is hard for them to take the gospel seriously. But if their Christian neighbours, the little flock in that village, are visibly finding joy in believing, rejoicing in God's forgiving grace, struggling to express in their lives the love and justice of God, then the others are far more likely to hear and be attracted to the message which has shown that it can transform lives. The congregation, the Body, the church is thus a kind of hermeneutic of the gospel. The message and the ethics are inseparable from the life of the church.

Within the Body hostility, suspicion, competition are pathological and can destroy its vitality and integrity. Yet the unity and harmony of the Body do not remove particularity, plurality and difference; indeed, these are enhanced and enriched and blended into a common purpose. In Christ the old animosities and separations, as exemplified in the classic division between Jew and Gentile, are overcome. The writer of the Letter to the Ephesians addresses the good news to the Gentiles:

> Once you were far off, but now in union with Jesus Christ you have been brought near through the shedding of Christ's blood. For he is himself our peace. Gentiles and Jews, he has made the two one, and in his own body of flesh and blood has broken down the barrier of enmity which separated them; for he annulled the law with its rules and regulations, so as to create out of the two a single new humanity in himself, thereby making peace. This was his purpose, to reconcile the two in a single body to God through the cross, by which he killed the enmity (Eph. 2:13-16).

Notice that God's purpose is to create a single new humanity. The unity of the church is simply a sign and foretaste of the broader unity of humankind which is God's goal. The unity of the church is therefore not something sought for its own sake — a matter, perhaps, of streamlining church structures, although any community needs organization if it is to survive and flourish. The New Testament teaches that the way the church is structured and operates is to be at the service of the gospel and to confirm that gospel. The church points to and already expresses in a partial way the coming unity of humankind.

Nor is the unity of the church seen only as a prerequisite for the church's mission, though it is that, too: in his "high priestly prayer" in John's gospel Jesus prays, "I ask... that they may all be one. As you, Father, are in me and I am in you, may they also be in us, so that the world may believe that you have sent me" (John 17:20-21). Unity is the goal as well as the way.

The unity of the church is therefore a vital expression of the gospel, a demonstration of the truth of the gospel. But there are true and phoney kinds of unity. Unity takes many forms. There is cheap unity as well as costly unity.

Church and ethics in the early centuries

In the centuries of Christendom the idea became commonly accepted that Christianity is the glue that binds society together, that it expresses a tradition with deep roots in the past, that it normally supports established authority and encourages obedience to the powers that be and that it is the ideological arm of government. Early "Christendom theologians" such as Eusebius saw a perfect harmony between church and state, and regarded them as mutually supportive, virtually mirror images of one another, both direct expressions of God's grace and providence. Far later, as Christendom was beginning to break up, it was still possible for a thinker like the English theologian Richard Hooker (1554-1600) to teach that the whole community belonged to both the church and the civil society, and to see no problem with the civil sovereign also being head of the church. The church and the state were simply two ways of looking at the same community: to be a reliable, loyal citizen it was necessary to be a baptized member of the church, and a central part of being a Christian was unquestioning loyalty to the established authorities.

It was not always like that. Early Christians often saw themselves as belonging to a kind of counterculture which was quite distinct from the earthly society in which they found themselves and which in a real sense anticipated the coming kingdom. The church represented an alternative to the existing social orders, which were believed to be rushing towards destruction. In the church a different and distinct ethics was recognized, a different hope was nurtured and a higher loyalty acknowledged. Tertullian, for instance, proclaimed:

> We are a body knit together as such by a common religious profession, by unity of discipline and by the bond of a common hope... We pray, too, for the emperors, for their ministers and for all in authority, for the welfare of the world, for the prevalence of peace, for the delay of the final consummation... Your citizenship, your magistracies, and the very name of your curia is the church of Christ... You are an alien in this world, and a citizen of the city of Jerusalem that is above. [1]

Within the church, Christians live by gospel standards. These are quite distinct from the ethics of the world and depend on the expectation of the end — for the delaying of which Christians pray. The church is a kind of parallel community which represents a challenge to the secular order because it stands as an alternative possibility of ordering life, the "still more excellent way" of love that Paul commends in 1 Corinthians 13.

It has been argued that it was this distancing from the world in order to sustain a fellowship of love without compromises with power which enabled Christianity to revitalize both community and social and political thought in late antiquity. The Christian community understood itself as the soul giving life to the body politic and sustaining that body by its prayers. But it was also a challenge to the state and a source of new and much-needed ideas for Western social thought. [2] It resisted assimilating its ethics to the dominant mores of the surrounding society, and it endeavoured to witness to the truth of the gospel and the value of the even better way of love in the way the community was structured and operated as well as in the words and actions of its members.

Church and ethics in the modern world

The Reformation and Enlightenment heralded the breakup of Christendom, now so apparent around the world. Once again the relation of the church and society is a matter of vigorous debate. Some argue that within a modern pluralist secular society the church should continue more or less as before, and be willing and able to address "the world" in the world's language. Others suggest that post-modernity is a crisis of moral and social fragmentation, a new dark ages full of dangers and threats. Just as the church sustained a renewed tradition of civility through the first dark ages, its task may be the same today. Alasdair MacIntyre discerns a massive contemporary crisis of community; and in his conclusion to his *After Virtue* he draws an analogy between the present and the collapse of the Roman empire and the start of the dark ages, when men and women of good will ceased to identify the continuance of civility and moral community with the propping up of the Roman *imperium:*

> What they set themselves to achieve instead — often not recognizing fully what they were doing — was the construction of new forms of community within which the moral life could be maintained so that both morality and civility might survive the coming ages of barbarism and darkness... For some time now we too have reached that turning point. What matters at this stage is the construction of local forms of community within which civility and the intellectual and moral life can be sustained through the new dark ages that are already upon us. And if the tradition of the virtues was able to survive the horrors of the last dark ages, we are not entirely without grounds for hope. This time, however, the barbarians are not waiting beyond the frontiers; they have already been governing us for quite some time. And it is our consciousness of this that constitutes part of our predicament. We are waiting not for a Godot, but for another — doubtless very different — St Benedict. [3]

MacIntyre's sombre vision has its attractions, and many people regard him as having put his finger on the contemporary predicament. Others feel that he is counselling retreat from the world, passivity, nostalgia and irresponsibility. But if the local communities in which he puts his trust might be Christian communities, it is important to note that they do not *voluntarily* decide to withdraw from influence over and interest in power; they are progressively excluded as the tradition is increasingly marginalized, and now they face a new situation, with its opportunities and dangers. Their new position at the margins need not lead to passivity, despair or nostalgia. They are more than stewards of a tradition; they reappropriate and renew the tradition and relate it to a quite new context.

Such communities are not bolt-holes for the timid and the backward-looking. By their very existence, by the way they structure their common life, by the nature of their celebrations, they make a constructive protest against the established order, "the rule of the barbarians". They are demonstrations of the viability of another way; insistently, they question by their very existence the adequacy of the community and culture in which they are set. They point to a better way, and are themselves signs, instruments and partial manifestations of the reign of God.

Furthermore, they are fellowships of expectation, aware of their own incompleteness and provisionality and brokenness. Unlike utopian communes they know that they are incapable by themselves of building Jerusalem or establishing the justice of God. They *wait*. But this is not a totally open and vacuous expectancy; nor do they already know and possess what is to come. They await a person, "a new — and doubtless very different — St Benedict". The first St Benedict made no attempt to claim the heart of things, to control the levers of power. Monasticism spoke truth from the margins. And so it may be today. Once again the church may witness at the margins. That great modern saint Thomas Merton saw the monk as a kind of parable of the Christian in the modern world. Monks, he wrote, "are people who have consciously and deliberately adopted a way of life which is marginal with respect to the rest of society, implicitly critical of that society, seeking a certain distance from that society and a freedom from its domination and its imperatives, but nevertheless open to its needs and in dialogue with it".[4] The monk "withdraws deliberately to the margins of society with

a view to deepening fundamental human experience".[5] At
the margins the monk experiences the depth and complexity
and confusion of the human condition today, but does not
give way to despair because the margin, the desert, the
wilderness is also the place where hope is discerned.

Even at the margins one waits not alone, but in fellowship with the *una sancta*, which is shaped by and nurtures the
ever-fresh tradition, that is the Body of Christ in space and
time. And the waiting that is enjoined, while it may exclude
participation in the "barbarian polity" on its own terms, is
active rather than passive. It involves exploration and experiment, hard thought and risky action, in community and
virtue and costly protest against evil, injustice and oppression.

The analysis of the world presented by the Czech president and former dissident Vaclav Havel is not far different
from that of MacIntyre. Havel saw the terminal agonies of
the Marxist regimes of Central and Eastern Europe as a
symptom of a far more profound and pervasive global
upheaval with its epicentre in Europe. Both East and West,
he argued, are simply variant forms of consumerist industrial
society. The old communist regimes were "a kind of warning
to the West, revealing its own latent tendencies".[6] The East
holds up a mirror to the West. Both are consumerist societies
in a deep crisis. In both the barbarians have taken over, and
everything is in disarray:

> A person who has been seduced by the consumer value system,
> whose identity is dissolved in an amalgam of its accoutrements
> of mass civilization, and who has no roots in the order of being,
> no sense of anything higher than his or her own personal
> survival, is a demoralized person; the system depends on his
> own demoralization, deepens it, is in fact a projection of it into
> society.[7]

The system — and Havel clearly means both the old
Marxist systems, where decadence, decay and dehumaniza-
tion were easy to discern, and the societies of the West,
where decline is more concealed — depends on *ideology*,

whose function "is to provide people... with the illusion that the system is in harmony with the human order and the order of the universe". Ideology legitimates power, for it pervasively suggests that "the centre of power is identical with the centre of truth".[8] Ideology — overtly in the old Marxist societies, more covertly elsewhere — is thus the main pillar of the system which effectively creates and internalizes a false reality: "It is built upon lies. It works only as long as people are willing to live within the lie."[9]

Thus, Havel suggests, most of us are living within the lie. But it is possible, even in a totalitarian dictatorship, for individuals or groups to live in the truth, rejecting the lie, exploding the ideological justification of oppression by shouting that the emperor has no clothes. The person who steps out of living within the lie — always a costly move — "rejects the ritual and breaks the rules of the game. He discovers once again his suppressed identity and dignity, he gives his freedom a concrete significance."[10] The truth is inherently a challenge to the system of lies. It involves a deep commitment to the priority of people over systems, any system. The task, Havel suggests, is dissent, resistance:

> It seems to me that all of us, East and West, face one fundamental task from which all else should follow. That task is one of resisting vigilantly, thoughtfully and attentively, but at the same time with total dedication, at every step and everywhere, the irrational momentum of anonymous, impersonal and inhuman power — the power of ideologies, systems, *apparat*, bureaucracy, artificial languages and political slogans. We must resist their complex and wholly alienating pressure, whether it takes the form of consumption, advertising, repression, technology or cliché — all of which are blood brothers of fanaticism and the wellspring of totalitarian thought.[11]

Dissent, resistance is the way to challenge the hegemony of lies, perhaps the only way in a fallen world to live in truth.

This idea of living in the truth, abiding in truth, dwelling in truth, as developed in recent times by Havel and by Michael Polanyi, is attractive as an account of the Christian life and the life of the church. Living in truth is not and cannot be an individual affair. It involves solidarity. And the community that lives in truth cannot be introverted, partial, *incurvatus in se*. There must be an element of universality and openness to it. So the community, according to Havel, "must foreshadow a general salvation and, thus, it is not just the expression of an introverted, self-contained responsibility that individuals have to and for themselves alone, but responsibility to and for the *world*". [12] This community is accordingly a parallel society, an alternative way of life. But it is not a ghetto, for the very notion of living within the truth is inescapably concerned with others. The community is responsible for the world and for those who are not its members: "Responsibility is ours... we must accept and grasp it *here, now*, in this place in time and space where the Lord has set us down." [13] Thus the parallel *polis* points beyond itself and only makes sense as an act of deepening one's responsibility to and for the whole, not as a way of escaping from responsibility.

And this community which lives in truth, dissents, resists, explores, represents an alternative *polis* and a different way of life is also open to the future. But unlike the ideological systems in which it is set, it does not sacrifice the present, or people, to the realization of the future, Indeed, it believes that the future is already present in a real, if partial, sense. It can be grasped and lived in the present inasfar as one lives in truth. "The real question", writes Havel, "is whether the 'brighter' future is already always so distant. What if, on the contrary, it has been here for a long time already, and only our own blindness and weakness have prevented us from seeing it around us and within us, and kept us from developing it?" [14]

What Havel and MacIntyre and Merton are saying points to ways of being church more characteristic of the early church than of the mainline churches during the centuries of Christendom. It may also be the seedbed for a style of believing and way of life which call for a certain kind of theology. This is not an ideology which authorizes systems

12

of power by linking them to the divine order. It has less to do with internalizing obedience and reverence for the system than with sparking off questioning, dissent, resistance. Unlike ideology and grand systems of thought which appear to explain everything with their overarching interpretations, this kind of theology is usually unscientific and unsystematic — fragments, hints, clues, cries, questions, pointers, protests and comments generated by the endeavour to live in the truth and do the truth and the acknowledgment that the truth cannot be manipulated, controlled, comprehended and captured, but only loved and lived in and revered and worshipped. And those who strive to dwell in the truth are sustained by the hope that today's "puzzling reflections in a mirror", dimly will at the end be replaced by a face-to-face encounter with the truth.

NOTES

[1] Tertullian, *Apologeticus* 39; *De Corona* 13.
[2] See Sheldon Wolin, *Politics and Vision*, London, Allen & Unwin, 1961, pp.96f.
[3] Alasdair MacIntyre, *After Virtue*, London, Duckworth, 1981, pp.244f.
[4] Cited in Kenneth Leech, *The Social God*, London, Sheldon, 1981, p.47.
[5] *Ibid.*, p.46.
[6] Vaclav Havel, *Living in Truth*, London, Faber, 1987, p.54.
[7] *Ibid.*, p.62.
[8] *Ibid.*, p.39.
[9] *Ibid.*, p.50.
[10] *Ibid.*, p.55.
[11] *Ibid.*, p.153.
[12] *Ibid.*, p.103.
[13] *Ibid.*, p.104.
[14] *Ibid.*, p.118.

2. Cheap or Costly Unity?

Costly grace

The martyr-theologian Dietrich Bonhoeffer wrote movingly of "costly grace". We have, he argued, cheapened grace. It is true that grace is a free gift of God, but it calls for a response from us that is neither cheap nor easy. Years before, John Newton caught the heart of the matter, although in characteristically individualist terms, in his famous hymn:

> Amazing grace (how sweet the sound!)
> that saved a wretch like me!
> I once was lost, but now am found,
> was blind, but now I see.
>
> 'Twas grace that taught my heart to fear,
> and grace my fears relieved;
> How precious did that grace appear
> the hour I first believed!

Newton realized that grace is not a static state of bliss: it comes to us in the midst of pilgrimage and struggle, pain and suffering, in the life of discipleship in company with others, in lives that are lived in the hope of the city that is to come, whose builder and maker is God:

> Through many dangers, toils and snares,
> I have already come;
> Tis grace has brought me safe thus far,
> and grace will lead me home.
>
> The Lord has promised good to me,
> his word my hope secures;
> he will my shield and portion be
> as long as life endures.

This grace calls us to hard pilgrimage, to costly discipleship. It elicits and enables a life of faith and love in solidarity with others. "Such grace", writes Bonhoeffer, "is *costly* because it calls us to follow, and it is *grace* because it calls us to follow Jesus Christ... Above all, it is *costly* because it cost God the life of his Son." [1] It is infinitely costly to God; and it is costly to disciples also, because it calls them to take on the yoke of Christ, whose yoke is easy and whose burden is light (Matt. 11:30).

Yet, Bonhoeffer argued, we have cheapened grace by separating it from the life of discipleship, by wrenching it apart from the cross, by sentimentality, by forgetting that it is the grace of our Lord Jesus Christ, who calls us to follow in the ways of grace and love and faithfulness even when the going gets rough — indeed, especially in the midst of opposition, conflict, suffering and hostility. Cheap grace leaves us — and the church, and the world — unchanged. It is a phoney grace which lubricates things as they are, which makes us content with ourselves and our situation. Costly grace provokes divine discontent. It transforms and reconciles and heals. It calls to discipleship and draws us into fellowship with God and with the vast and variegated host of those for whom God cares, especially the weak and the poor and the oppressed. It is, in T.S. Eliot's words in "Little Gidding":

> A condition of complete simplicity
> (Costing not less than everything).

Cheap and costly unity

Unity likewise is that strange thing, a costly gift. It is both totally gratuitous and deeply demanding. It has been won for us by Christ on the cross, who absorbed and overcame forever the powerful forces of disunity, hostility, contempt, suspicion, injustice and oppression. He welcomes us into the unity and *shalom* that he has gained for us and for all humankind. But he does not coerce us into unity. Those who were once separate have been brought near in the blood of Christ; the "dividing wall of hostility", like the Berlin wall, has been broken down forever; the paradigmatic division between Jew and Gentile has been overcome; and thus a new community of conviviality and harmony for all has been established:

> So then you are no longer strangers and aliens, but you are citizens with the saints and also members of the household of God, built upon the foundation of the apostles and prophets, with Christ Jesus himself as the cornerstone. In him the whole

structure is joined together and grows into a holy temple in the Lord; in whom you also are built together spiritually into a dwelling place for God (Eph. 2:19-22).

Like grace, this unity is a precious gift which requires a costly response. Although it has been achieved for us by Christ, we need to demonstrate its reality in a world that is still full of division, conflict, suspicion and hostility. We need to live out the unity and *shalom* that Christ has won. We must become the people and the communities that we already are in Christ. And this is not easy, for it means going against the stream, resisting the way of the world, marching to the beat of a different drum. There is resistance inside us — the sinfulness of the old humanity. And all of us have a deep-seated fear of the new and the strange and the alien. These things need to be faced and wrestled with and overcome if we are to move forward into the fullness of unity that Christ offers us. Unity cannot be had without taking risks. But the life of faith is a life of risk-taking.

"Cheap unity avoids morally contested issues because they would disturb the unity of the church."[2] It strives to sustain a brittle and superficial fellowship by plastering over deep-seated disagreements, so that the peace of the church is maintained at the expense of its relevance and honesty. Costly unity is the discovery or rediscovery of the churches' unity in struggles for peace and justice. Even in open, frank and vigorously contested debate about moral issues a lively sense of unity can often develop. In the South African struggle, for example, the unity that is given in Christ was often encountered in the solidarity of witness and social praxis.[3]

Christian unity

Christians believe that the church is called to exemplify the unity and harmony, the reconciliation and justice that have been won for us by Christ. Its task is to show, in a bitterly divided world, the reality of what Christ has done, to demonstrate God's purposes for all humankind. The church stands in the midst of deep-seated conflicts to show that hostilities can be and have been overcome, that reconciliation is a reality. The being of the church, its inner life and its outward organization, should confirm and exemplify the gospel that it preaches.

But only too often divided churches mirror the divisions of the world, and sometimes even make them worse. Often the actual life of the Christian community seems to be in no way distinctive; and sometimes the behaviour and community life of Christians are in fact a scandal, because there is such an obvious discrepancy between the faith they profess and the way they believe, between what they say and signify in worship and what they do the rest of the time.

Often enough Christians have been content with a superficial and undemanding idea of unity, which does not plumb the depths of the human condition or engage with the deep roots of conflict, oppression and injustice. There has been too much "band-aid unity", which suggests a superficial, quick and easy healing of wounds and divisions which are in reality ancient and deeply rooted. Christians frequently seek forms of unity which involve the minimum of change, which do not challenge or disturb entrenched patterns of belief and practice. These cost very little, and suggest that church unity is a matter of cobbling together denominations, not unlike the amalgamation of two businesses to improve their efficiency, or the union of two clubs when there are not enough members to go round. Sociologists have suggested that the ecumenical movement is just that — churches huddling ever closer in an increasingly hostile environment, like sheep trying to survive in a snowstorm. There is some truth in this theory. But it is also true that the search for unity is often most vigorous where the churches are growing fastest, and are most lively. The search for true unity must be costly, disturbing and demanding. And it is also renewing.

Costly unity can come only when the sources of conflict, distrust, injustice and violence — many times centuries-old grievances which constantly refresh bitterness — are addressed and wrestled with and gradually healed at their source. It is memories as well as present conflicts that call for healing. Grievances and injustices, past and present, are real, deep and living, and demand repentance, restitution, and ultimately forgiveness and healing. And all these are hard and costly.

The unity of the church and the unity of humankind

Superficial and glib talk about unity and reconciliation, calling simplistically for instant harmony, merely plasters over the cracks and disguises real conflicts of interest. Often it is used as a cover for sordid settlements imposed by the powerful in their own interests. The Kairos document reminded us, before the collapse of the apartheid regime in South Africa, that conflicts need to be recognized and worked through painfully and with integrity. Martin Luther King and other leaders in the US civil rights movement, like Mahatma Gandhi in India, showed how difficult and costly and how important it is to right wrongs, establish justice, heal antagonisms and overcome conflicts of interest while simultaneously realizing a broader and more authentic sense of community.

The Kairos document accused what it called "church theology" of trivializing conflict by suggesting that differences are based simply on misunderstandings, which can be fairly easily resolved so that instant unity and reconciliation are always possible. "Church theology" denies that most conflicts have deep roots in situations of injustice which must be remedied and put right if reconciliation is to be actualized. Repentance, restitution and the establishment of justice are necessary for true unity:

> In our situation in South Africa today it would be totally un-Christian to plead for reconciliation and peace before the present injustices have been removed. Any such plea plays into the hands of the oppressor by trying to persuade those of us who are oppressed to accept our oppression and to become reconciled to the intolerable crimes that are committed against us. This is not Christian reconciliation; it is asking us to become accomplices in our own oppression, to become ser-

vants of the devil. No reconciliation is possible in South Africa without justice.

What this means in practice is that no reconciliation, no forgiveness and no negotiations are possible *without repentance...* [4]

There is thus a false, but seductive, unity and a true unity. False unity compromises the truth, and covers over injustice and oppression. It freezes existing structures of injustice and oppression. True unity rests on repentance, truth, justice and love. It is costly because it demands change, transformation, restitution, conversion; it unmasks and confronts the forces of evil and division rather than compromising or colluding with them.

"Church theology", the Kairos theologians continue, sits on the fence. It issues calls for unity and reconciliation and for nonviolence. While its pronouncements appear to condemn all violence impartially, they are in practice far more stringent on the despairing violent response of the oppressed than on the ruthless and sustained violence of the state apparatus. In making a virtue of even-handedness, "church theology" in fact gives tacit support to the oppressor. It is critical of systemic and divisive injustice in a limited and guarded way; its dominant concern is to safeguard the church as an institution, thus making it cautious about any action or statement which might endanger the position of the church. "Church theology" was thus also critical of apartheid in a guarded and cautious way. It is diplomatic and nervous, preferring to appeal to the powerful rather than confront directly the forces of injustice and division. Church leaders are reluctant to put a strain on the existing unity of their churches, fragile and limited as this is, even when this is the price of reaching forward to embrace a fuller, more authentic unity.

The Kairos document advocates what it calls "prophetic theology". This is a response to the situation which is biblical, spiritual, pastoral and prophetic. It is a call to action that arises from discerning the signs of the times in the light of the Bible and of careful social analysis. It is a summons to repentance, conversion and change. It is a proclamation of the good news of salvation:

> It will *denounce* sin and *announce* salvation... Our theology must name the sins and the evils that surround us and the salvation we are hoping for. Prophecy must name the sins of apartheid, injustice, oppression and tyranny in South Africa today as an offence against God and the measures which must be taken to overcome these sins and the suffering that they cause. On the other hand, prophecy will announce the hopeful good news of future liberation, justice and peace, as God's will and promise, naming the ways of bringing this about and encouraging people to take action.[5]

Prophetic theology is always a message of hope and of encouragement for the oppressed. It is a challenge not simply to the forces of oppression and injustice, but also to the church. It calls the church to *be* the church, showing in its life the justice, reconciliation and unity that it proclaims and seeks in the world. The church is to be a kind of earnest of God's purposes for all humankind, a demonstration of the truth of the gospel. And this challenge calls the churches to a radical renewal with a restoration of unity at its heart. Such unity is not a matter of administrative convenience or organizational efficiency. It is an essential part of the church's witness to the gospel. Only so may the church be a sign or sacrament of God's purpose of unity for all humankind.

Costly unity

A World Council of Churches consultation held in Rønde, Denmark, in 1993 produced a report entitled "Costly Unity". Moral issues and struggles, the report declared, often mark the distinction between cheap and costly unity: "Cheap unity avoids morally contested issues because they would disturb the unity of the church. Costly unity is discovering the churches' unity as a gift of pursuing justice and peace."[6] In the struggle for Namibian independence and the struggle against apartheid in South Africa, state authorities made strenuous and partly successful attempts to use the classic principle of "divide and conquer" and play off one Christian denomination against another in order to weaken the opposition to unjust regimes. These efforts betrayed a clear recognition that in unity lies strength. As Archbishop Desmond Tutu repeated often, apartheid was too strong for divided churches; and in the course of the struggles against it there was often a new experience of unity, new ecumenical ground was sometimes broken. Lesser loyalties to nation or ethnic or class group were transcended, and there was a lively experience that in Christ the dividing walls are broken down, that we are reconciled to God and to one another. This is "the unity of the church accomplished on the way of the cross, paid for by the life of the martyrs, whose witness inevitably included moral witness".[7] In moral struggle a new unity has been discovered, a costly, gracious unity. "Its enemy is cheap unity — forgiveness without repentance, baptism without discipleship, life without daily dying and rising in a household of faith... that is to be the visible sign of God's desire for the whole inhabited earth."[8] Others have found that involvement in the conciliar process for Justice, Peace and the Integrity of Creation has been for them a profound experience of what it is to be "church". Indeed some would go so far as to say that "the human moral struggle, with all its pressures, sorrows and hopes, is a basic ecclesiogenetic power";[9] in other words, the church grows as much through moral struggle as from doctrinal clarification or explicit evangelism. A central concern with ethical stances is inseparable from what it is to be church.

But it is not easy to articulate the relation between moral commitment and the church clearly and precisely. In moral struggles Christians commonly experience a deep solidarity with many who are outside the fellowship of the church, and often have no apparent desire for Christian faith. Rønde suggested controversially that "it is not too much to say that the holiness of the church means the constant moral struggle of its members";[10] others have spoken of specific moral commitments as being part of the *esse* of the church — essential components of what it is to be church. But many look on such statements as an undue moralizing of the

Christian faith and of the church, as if the church is not so much a community of forgiven sinners as a company of moral heroes, drawn into fellowship not so much by grace as by shared moral commitments and struggles. Yet the experience of learning from those who are not Christians what it is to be church and what the gospel calls us to do is a common one today and has to be taken into account.

Something like a consensus was emerging that the faith and worship of the church necessarily involve moral commitments, some of which are so central that those who do not share them cannot be part of the fellowship. At the individual level there is nothing particularly novel in this concern. From the beginnings of the Christian church flagrant and persistent immorality has been seen as a ground for exclusion from the community and has been commonly associated with heresy. Donald MacKinnon has explored the question whether notoriously immorality like Paul Tillich's womanizing or Gerhard Kittel's antisemitism should qualify the seriousness with which we regard their theology.[11] But the notion of moral heresy so severe that it necessitates a breach of fellowship and the exclusion of the offending group from the church or the ecumenical movement is a comparatively recent development, which has particularly been associated with the great 20th-century issues of Nazism and the Holocaust, apartheid, and now more generally with attitudes towards the environment and issues of economic justice.

The German church struggle

Dietrich Bonhoeffer recognized early on that the German church struggle would be a decisive stage in the development of the ecumenical movement and would to a large extent determine its future. He was also one of the first to recognize that the primary issue in that struggle was neither the organizational freedom of the church nor even its ability to successfully resist the "Aryan clause", which prohibited the ordination of ministers of Jewish descent, but rather the onslaught against the Jews and other vulnerable minorities which culminated in the Holocaust. What happened in and to the

German church was of vital concern to the whole *oikoumene*, and other churches could not but involve themselves in the struggle. To decide to stand aloof on the sidelines was itself to make a powerful theological and moral statement, a declaration about what it was to be "church".

Bonhoeffer recognized that many church people from around the world began for the first time to see the reality of the ecumenical movement in the context of the German church struggle, and found their own understanding of what it was to be church enlarged and challenged. Ecumenical leaders were able to see that in the struggle of the Confessing Church the integrity of the Christian faith and the Christian church was deeply implicated, and that "the struggle has been brought to a head and undergone by the Confessing Church vicariously for all Christianity, and particularly for Western Christianity". [12] With a new solidarity among churches opposed to Nazism in the ecumenical movement a fresh awareness of what it meant to be the *oikoumene* emerged. This involved a lively sense of mutual accountability. Bonhoeffer wrote:

> In this encounter the ecumenical movement and the Confessing Church ask each other the reason for their existence. The ecumenical movement must vindicate itself before the Confessing Church and the Confessing Church must vindicate itself before the ecumenical movement, and just as the ecumenical movement is led to a serious inward concern and crisis by the Confessing Church, so too the Confessing Church is led to a serious inward concern and crisis by the ecumenical movement. The reciprocal questioning must now be developed. [13]

The Confessing Church confronts the ecumenical movement in the first place with its confession, the doctrinal stance it has been forced to take — like Luther declaring, "Here I stand. I can do no other. So help me God." Its ethical positions are not so much consequences which flow from the confession, or implications of the confession, as something integral to the doctrinal stance. Here doctrine *is* ethics, and ethical action is inseparable from doctrinal confession. And here neutrality is impossible; one has to say yes or no. Whichever choice one makes one is taking a stand which is both ethical and doctrinal. And in affirming the confession one is declaring those who reject it to be in heresy.

The confession which is constitutive of the true church, and which has its indispensable ethical component, is simultaneously a basis for unity and a cause of division. One cannot stand both with the Confessing Church and with the German Christians. One has to make a choice. And here "living confession does not mean the putting of one dogmatic thesis up against another; it means a confession in which it is really a matter of life or death. A naturally formulated, clear, theologically based, true confession. But theology itself is not the fighting part here; it stands wholly at the service of the living, confessing and struggling church."[14] Yet the Confessing Church, while striving to dwell in truth, shares in the guilt for the brokenness of Christianity and the false theologies against which it protests: "it shudders before the gravity of a cleavage in the church and before the burden it is laying on subsequent generations".[15] However, it can do no other.

Unity and division

Thus in the German church struggle, as in the struggle against apartheid and in other similar acute historical crises, there is on the one hand a renewed and enlarged understanding of what the church is and what real community involves, and on the other hand a recognition that painful separation and division are unavoidable. As we have seen, the German Confessing Church discovered the importance of confession and recognized that taking an ethical stance is central to it. It also found in a new way that it was part of the world church, dependent on other branches of the church for support and understanding and questioning. Within the world church different branches had to give an account of themselves to one another; they were responsible to God and to one another. And they were responsible not only for their own inner life, but for the broader communities in which they were set.

From the start of his work, Bonhoeffer was centrally concerned with the church as community. His doctoral dissertation, published as *Sanctorum Communio* (1927), explored the church as "Christ existing in community". *The Cost of Discipleship* discussed the costly commitment that was at the heart of a community of disciples. And Bonhoeffer's work at the Confessing Church seminary in Finkenwald, so movingly reflected in his *Life Together,* was a practical experiment in being the church. In this situation, being the true church necessarily involved separation from and denunciation of the German Christians as a false church. But one did not confess the faith simply to protect one's own or one's church's purity and integrity and faithfulness. Bonhoeffer had a passionate solidarity both with the true church and with the destiny of his people, the German people. When in 1939 he went to New York at the invitation of Reinhold Niebuhr and others, who were concerned for his safety after the outbreak of war, he quickly realized he had made a mistake and decided to return. He wrote to Niebuhr to explain his decision:

> I must live through this difficult period of our national life with the Christian people of Germany. I will have no right to participate in the reconstruction of Christian life in Germany after the war if I do not share the trials of this time with my people... Christians in Germany will face the dreadful alternative of either willing the defeat of their nation in order that Christian civilization may survive, or willing the victory of their nation and thereby destroying our civilization. I know which of these alternatives I must choose; but I cannot make that choice in security. [16]

The faithfulness and integrity of Christians and of the church were of vital importance for the German nation. The Confessing Church was not to be a ghetto, isolated from the life of the nation. God loved the nation, and called it also to serve God's purposes. Bonhoeffer and his colleagues were German patriots in the truest sense, and knew that God cared for the German people. [17] Their faithfulness as Christians and the faithfulness of the Confessing Church were the best and truest service to the German people and the German nation in their time of crisis. A central aspect of this faithfulness was their unity with the church outside Germany, a unity which was costly and which paradoxically made division within the German church inevitable. Like the wheat and the tares in the parable, Christian unity and Christian division mysteriously grow together in a fallen, broken world. The road to unity is sometimes the painful way of division as we reach forward to the unity in truth and love which is God's purpose.

NOTES

[1] Dietrich Bonhoeffer, *The Cost of Discipleship*, London, SCM, 1948, p.39.
[2] Thomas F. Best and Wesley Granberg-Michaelson, eds, *Costly Unity: Koinonia and Justice, Peace and Creation*, Geneva, WCC, 1993, p.88.
[3] See John de Gruchy, "Koinonia and the Ecumenical Church: Perspectives from South Africa", in Thomas F. Best and Gunther Gassmann eds, *On the Way to Fuller Koinonia: Official Report of the Fifth World Conference on Faith and Order*, Geneva, WCC, 1994, pp.37ff.
[4] "The Kairos Document", London, CIIR and BCC, 2nd ed., 1986, p.10.
[5] *Ibid.*, p.18.
[6] Best and Granberg-Michaelson, *op. cit.*, p.88.
[7] *Ibid.*
[8] *Ibid.*
[9] Cf. A. Houtepen, *ibid.*, p.6.
[10] *Ibid.*, p.87.
[11] See "Tillich, Frege, Kittel: Some Reflections on a Dark Theme", in Donald MacKinnon, *Explorations in Theology — 5*, London, SCM, 1979, pp.129-37.
[12] Dietrich Bonhoeffer, *No Rusty Swords: Letters, Lectures, and Notes from the Collected Works*, London, Collins, 1965, p.327.
[13] *Ibid.*, pp.328f.
[14] *Ibid.*, p.338.

[15] *Ibid.*, p.338.

[16] D. Bonhoeffer, *The Way to Freedom: Letters, Lectures and Notes, 1935-1939*, ed. E.H. Robertson, New York, Harper, 1966, p.246.

[17] See Keith Clements' spendid discussion of this theme in *A Patriotism for Today: Love of Country in Dialogue with the Witness of Dietrich Bonhoeffer*, London, Collins, 1986.

3. Ethics and Ecumenism: A Journey Together

From its beginnings the modern ecumenical movement has wrestled with the relation between ethics and the being and unity of the church. There has been a steady conviction that there *is* a relationship, but spelling out what it is has continued to prove difficult and controversial. Some people have felt that the only way to progress towards unity is either to set aside ethical concerns, which are so often divisive among Christians, or at least to pursue the two quests independently of one another. Others have found in ethical struggles a new and vital experience of unity and solidarity, even of what it means to be the church, or new and challenging ethical insights emerging from the work of the ecumenical movement and the new experiences of unity that this has brought. In this chapter we look at some of the key moments in this ecumenical quest for a fuller understanding of what it is to be the church of Jesus Christ and of the ethics involved in discipleship in unity.

From its early days, the modern ecumenical movement has had three strands, concerned respectively with the Christian world mission, Christian witness in the social, economic and political spheres, and the issues of doctrine and church order which have for centuries kept the churches apart. In some ways this simply represented a division of labour within what was generally recognized to be a common task. But the different responsibilities were entrusted to three more or less separate institutional structures: the International Missionary Council, the Life and Work movement (later the Church and Society unit of the World Council of Churches) and the Faith and Order Commission. Each pursued fairly distinct agendas, largely in separation from one another. Gradually the World Council of Churches became the coordinating body for all three activities. Faith and Order and Life and Work were absorbed into the WCC at its inception; the International Missionary Council became part of the WCC in 1961. Coordination between the three organizations was not always as good as it should have been, and there was a mounting awareness that separation introduced distortions and duplication, that there was a massive overlap and that the task ultimately was one. It was increasingly recognized that the search for unity was intimately related to the mission of the church, and that the struggle for peace and justice could not be separated from either.

Missionary beginnings

The landmark world missionary conference held in Edinburgh in 1910 is commonly recognized as "the birthplace of the modern ecumenical movement". [1] Official representatives of all the major Protestant and Anglican churches and missionary societies gathered for a conference which arose out of a mounting conviction that the world mission of the Christian church demanded unity and better coordination among the churches. In most of what were called the "younger churches" divisions which had been imported from Europe and North America made little sense, diverted effort from the task at hand and obscured the very message of reconciliation that was being preached. Edinburgh was essentially about cooperation and unity in a common task. It was a practically oriented gathering, which from the beginning set aside the doctrinal and ecclesiastical issues which divided Christians on the assumption that unity in mission and in service is possible even while these other matters are unresolved.

It had long since been discovered that competition in mission was harmful, diverting effort, wasting resources and duplicating activities in the same area. Thus in most mission fields there were long-standing "comity agreements", allocating different areas to the various societies and missions. But comity did not resolve the problem of disunity. Christians moving from one area to another found very different kinds of churches from those to which they had been accustomed. Often they were not even accepted as members of the church or admitted to the Lord's table. Local Christians expressed growing discontent at divisions which made little sense to them, and which seemed to contradict the gospel of reconciliation and unity that was preached. Later, as colonies struggled for independence, nation-building and the overcoming of deep-seated social conflicts, the divisions between Christian denominations often seemed not just irrelevant but offensive. Thus it was among the "younger churches" of Asia and Africa that the strongest pressures for church unity built up. The establishment in 1947 of the Church of South India, followed by church unions in a number of other Asian countries, was in a real sense a fruit of Edinburgh 1910.

While Edinburgh's primary focus was a practical one — developing a coordinated strategy for the churches' mission — this had, as we have seen, implications for church unity; and it did not prove possible to set aside for long the questions of theology and of church order which had been excluded from the conference's agenda. But Edinburgh 1910 also recognized that the mission of the church necessarily involved prophecy. Issues of justice, of peace and of social order could not ignored. So when in 1921 the Edinburgh Continuation Committee gave way to a new International Missionary Council (IMC), among its aims were included:

> to help unite Christian public opinion in support of freedom of conscience and religion and of missionary liberty;

> to help unite the Christian forces of the world in seeking justice in international and inter-racial relations. [2]

It is beyond the scope of this book to examine how far and how effectively the IMC in fact concerned itself with issues of peace, justice and freedom. The point is simply to note that from the beginning it picked up a note that had been rather cautiously sounded at Edinburgh: that these matters were an integral part of the mission of the church.

By the time of the next world missionary conference, held in Jerusalem in 1928, circumstances had radically changed. The liberal triumphalism that had characterized the 1910 conference had been undercut by the horrors of the first world war and its aftermath. This conference now saw the churches as embattled together against secularism, and charged with presenting the gospel to collectivities and nations as well as to individuals. "The gospel of Christ", the conference declared, "contains a message, not only for the individual soul, but for the world of social organization and economic relations in which individuals live."[3] Accordingly, a department of social and industrial research was established as part of the IMC, and it produced a series of influential and carefully researched reports on subjects such as forced labour, migrant labour and African marriage problems. Mission, all this implied, was inescapably tied to issues of justice in the world.

The IMC met again in 1938 at Tambaram, in South India. This time the proceedings were dominated by the threat of war and the ominous totalitarian spectre of Nazism and Stalinism. In the book written as a preparatory study for the meeting, *The Christian Message in a Non-Christian World*, Dutch theologian Hendrik Kraemer sharply distinguished the Christian revelation from the religions and ideologies of humankind, in a way reminiscent of the theology of Karl Barth. Kraemer's understanding of mission was confrontational: truth must denounce falsehood and lies, because these degrade and destroy people and social institutions. Beneath the surface of this approach to other faiths, which seemed to many to be arrogant and aggressive, lurked the conviction that Hitler and Stalin had shown the depth of evil to which false doctrine and idolatry lead. The conference, in addition to — or as part of — presenting a strategy for mission, condemned the invasion of a country by the armed forces of another, and declared that "justice requires the elimination of the domination of one people by another". It took a firm stand against antisemitism:

> We call upon the churches and individual Christians to do whatever is in their power to help in the solution of the acute and tragic world problem which has arisen as a result of the persecution of the Jewish race in many countries. We urge that Christians free themselves from race hatred and easy acquiescence in popular prejudices which lend unconscious support to such persecutions.[4]

The linkage between mission and unity was most dramatically affirmed at the Willingen meeting of the IMC after the second world war, in 1952. At this meeting the delegates from the "younger churches" declared:

> We believe that the unity of the churches is an essential condition of effective witness and advance. In the lands of the younger churches divided witness is a crippling handicap. We of the younger churches feel this very keenly. While unity may be desirable in the lands of the older churches it is *imperative* in those of the younger churches.

The whole conference responded by speaking of "the calling of the church to mission *and unity*":

> The love of God in Christ calls for the threefold response of worship, unity and mission. These three aspects of the church's response are interdependent; they become corrupted when isolated from each other. Division in the church distorts its witness, frustrates its mission and contradicts its own nature. If the church is to demonstrate the gospel in its life as well as in its preaching, it must manifest to the world the power of God to break down all barriers and establish the church's unity in Christ. *Christ is not divided.*[5]

Thus, the decision of the IMC to become part of the World Council of Churches in 1961 was a recognition that the concern with mission could not be separated from commitment to unity, or from the search for justice and peace in the social order.

Life and Work

The outbreak of the first world war in 1914 demonstrated for many socialists the impotence of the international solidarity of the working class in face of nationalism, and for many Christians the frailty of the new sense of unity and common purpose among Christian churches which had been represented at the Edinburgh conference of 1910. During the war there had been various attempts to organize collaborative projects among the churches for reconciliation and peacemaking, and after the war there was a renewed determination to work together. Among many people the conviction grew that whereas dogma divides, common service unites. Strenuous efforts to bring the churches together in shared practical work and engagement with the problems of society and of the economy gathered force. Just as the Edinburgh conference had ruled out debate on issues of doctrine and ecclesiology in order to concentrate on unity in mission, so, too, at the conference on Life and Work which finally gathered in Stockholm in 1925 it was assumed that the gospel message could best be addressed to the problems of the day if issues of doctrine and different understandings of the church were temporarily set aside.

The chief midwife of the Life and Work movement and chair of the Universal Christian Conference on Life and Work in Stockholm in 1925 was the Swedish archbishop Nathan Söderblom. He was a passionate advocate of the unity of the church, believing that a divided world needed to see the reconciling power of Christ manifested in a united church. He was deeply disturbed by the first world war, which demonstrated, he believed, "the spiritual treacheries and disasters involved in a war between professedly Christian nations". During the war he made a number of unsuccessful attempts at peace-making, and after the war he worked tirelessly for a closer cooperation between the churches in their work for peace and justice. The Stockholm conference was convened in order "to concentrate the mind of Christendom on the mind of Christ as revealed in the gospels towards those great social, industrial and international questions which are so acutely urgent in our civilization". [6] The Christian response could not be solely in terms of charity and social work; a prophetic note also needed to be sounded, which discerned the roots of social problems and pointed towards a cure. In action and in prophecy, in "the application of Christian ethics to the social problems of modern life", the fellowship between the churches would be strengthened, and they would grow towards unity.

Stockholm appointed a continuation committee, which in due course launched the Universal Christian Council for Life and Work. When its next conference was held in Oxford in 1937, the context was very different, with the rise of Hitler and the growth of Stalinism, and J.H. Oldham, the chief architect of the conference, declared that its main focus was "the life-and-death struggle between the Christian faith and the secular and pagan tendencies of our time".[7] The secularism that had been a main object of attention in the 1920s was now replaced with the new paganism, and the struggle accordingly became more acute and polarized. Behind the slogan associated with the conference — "Let the Church be the Church!" — lay a deep concern with the issues of the German church struggle, particularly as understood by Dietrich Bonhoeffer and Karl Barth. The issue was now seen less in terms of addressing a constructive word to the affairs of the world than of confronting the "principalities and powers" ranged so threateningly against the church and capable of subverting its integrity. No longer could practical and ethical issues be treated in isolation from issues of faith and of doctrine. The confrontation with the new paganism went right to the heart of the gospel. The being of the church was implicated in the struggle. Doctrine and ethics could not be held apart.

As W.A. Visser 't Hooft put it in one of the preparatory volumes for the Oxford conference:

> Churches are bodies which exist to proclaim the truth of God; and it is therefore their function, when they meet individually or together, to bear witness to the message which has been entrusted to them. Representatives of churches can never meet without at least attempting to live up to their main obligation, which is *to be the church*, and to announce the lordship of Christ over the world.[8]

In opposition to the powerful but false conceptions of state and of community, the church should affirm and demonstrate the existence of a "God-given community which transcends all human divisions, and that *as a reality*, and not merely as an ideal..." Only a united church would be able to give a fully adequate demonstration of the meaning of the church, as in it there would be the full fellowship of witness and sacraments in common.[9] The church that finds its embodiment in service and in sacrament must be united if it is to confirm the gospel that it preaches and manifest the fullness of community that is God's will for all.

The Oxford conference was thus inevitably drawn into taking a stand on the nature of the church and affirming — against the *Führerprinzip* — the lordship of Christ. The church, in Oldham's words,

> should be the place where barriers of race, nationality, class, sex and education are done away; where the unprivileged, the downtrodden, the outcast and the despised find a welcome and feel themselves at home; a meeting-ground where those who are divided in questions of politics and economics can realize afresh their unity in loyalty to a common Lord, can discuss their differences in the reality of their fellowship and learn mutually to understand one another. In the modern disintegration of social life the church ought to provide centres in which men [*sic*] can find protection, shelter and security in the care and love of their fellow-men, and re-discover the meaning of community in the support and comradeship of a society, the members of which bear one another's burdens and seek the good of all. The church ought also to be the place not only where support and encouragement are given to those who need it, but where the more robust and vigorous may find their individualism and self-will disciplined and tempered, and their purposes purified and strengthened in a common endeavour to learn and fulfil the will of Christ.[10]

In the light of a serious "discerning of the signs of the times" and a conviction that the lordship of Christ demands involvement in the social, political and economic issues of the day, Oxford found itself going beyond the traditional Life and Work limits and making affirmations about doctrine and the nature of the church. Conflict with "the new pagan tendencies" made it necessary to define what is incompatible with Christian faith, to talk about heresy and its evil practical outworkings and to draw a boundary around the church — themes that would later recur in the debates about apartheid and the world economic system. In engagement with the life and the problems of the world, the nature and the task of the church were clarified.

Faith and Order

At Edinburgh 1910, as we have seen, issues of doctrine and church order were regarded as potentially explosive and thus liable to make impossible the primary task of developing a cooperative strategy for mission. Indeed, the Anglo-Catholics were represented at Edinburgh only on the clear understanding that these matters, so sensitive for them, were kept off the agenda. But the Edinburgh conference power-fully stimulated a thirst for a unity which went far beyond cooperation and in so doing it thus ignited the modern quest for unity. It was clear to all intelligent observers that progress towards this goal depended on tackling directly the difficult issues of doctrine and church order which separated the major Christian traditions.

It was Bishop Charles H. Brent of the Episcopal Church in the USA who, with the support of his own denomination, took the lead in arranging a conference to address the "faith and order" issues which had been taboo at Edinburgh. Invitations to a world conference on faith and order were sent "to all Christian communions"; and when the conference assembled in Lausanne in 1927 all the main Protestant, Anglican and Orthodox churches were represented. Only the Roman Catholic Church emphatically turned down the invitation. Lausanne 1927, like Edinburgh and Stockholm before it, launched a movement for Christian unity which was independent until it became part of the new World Council of Churches. The remit of Faith and Order was to tackle the tricky and contentious issues of doctrine, worship and church order which were such obvious factors in church division. But Lausanne also gave some attention to ethical issues. It declared that the gospel is "the only way by which humanity can escape from those class and race hatreds which devastate society at present into the enjoyment of national well-being and international friendship and peace". [11] But as yet there was no serious attempt to relate issues of unity and division within the church to the life of the world with its tensions and possibilities.

Faith and Order was not expected to concern itself with questions of service, or with the great economic, social and international issues which faced the church. Such matters were seen as the responsibility of Life and Work. Nor was it concerned with mission — that was the task of the IMC. But gradually it became abundantly clear that this division was impossible to maintain. The unity of the church was not a matter of organizational convenience or a purely domestic concern for the churches. It had worldly and indeed cosmic significance. Nor could one properly separate the mission of the church from Faith and Order concerns. After all, Jesus had prayed that his followers might all be one precisely so that "the world may believe" that he was sent by God (John 17:21).

Thus questions of ethics began to loom large in the work of the Commission on Faith and Order, as it explored more and more deeply the implications of doctrine and worship for the world and for the search for justice and peace, as well as for the unity of the church. Much of this will be explored later in this book; at this point we shall mention just two landmark Faith and Order documents.

The first — *Baptism, Eucharist and Ministry* — represented a remarkable theological convergence on central issues which had long divided the churches, and its appearance in 1982 was the fruit of many years of painstaking work. At each point in this text the implications of what Christians say and do in worship and in the way they structure their churches are spelled out. Thus,

> as they grow in the Christian life of faith, baptized believers demonstrate that humanity can be regenerated and liberated. They have a common responsibility, here and now, to bear witness together to the gospel of Christ, the Liberator of all human beings. The context of this common witness is the church and the world. Christians... acknowledge that baptism,

as a baptism into Christ's death, has ethical implications which not only call for personal sanctification, but also motivate Christians to strive for the realization of the will of God in all realms of life. [12]

The eucharist, likewise, "opens up the vision of the divine rule which has been promised as the final renewal of creation, and is a foretaste of it". It "embraces all aspects of life", and "is a constant challenge in the search for appropriate relationships in social, economic and political life... All kinds of injustice, racism, separation and lack of freedom are radically challenged when we share in the body and blood of Christ" (Eucharist, paras 20,22).

And in the treatment of ministry, we are told that "the members of Christ's body are to struggle with the oppressed towards that freedom and dignity promised with the coming of the kingdom... In so doing they bring to the world a foretaste of the joy and glory of God's kingdom" (Ministry, para. 4).

Another influential document indicating this new Faith and Order emphasis is the fruit of a study on "the unity of the church and the renewal of humankind", [13] which dates back to the 1968 assembly of the WCC in Uppsala, which famously declared that "the church is bold in speaking of itself as the sign of the coming unity of [hu]mankind". The assembly had called for "a new openness to the world in its aspirations, its achievements, its restlessness and its despair" for sometimes the world's instruments of conciliation and peace-making seemed more effective than the churches themselves. The churches which denounce racism are sometimes themselves implicated in the very sins they denounce. It is necessary for the church to be renewed if it is indeed to be a sign of renewal and unity. The world and its needs call the church to renewal and unity; and the church in its mission to the world may be enriched and challenged by the world. [14] Unity and renewal belong together, and only a church which struggles seriously for its own unity and renewal is capable of being an effective and hopeful sign of unity to the world. This study therefore attempted, with much success, to hold together traditional concerns of Faith and Order and of Life and Work and to show their deep interdependence.

From Responsible Society to Justice, Peace and the Integrity of Creation

The inaugural assembly of the World Council at Amsterdam in 1948 held up the notion of the "Responsible Society" as the Christian ideal. The overall theme of the assembly was "Man's Disorder and God's Design", and there was a clear confidence that in the midst of the immense problems following the second world war the Christian churches not only had a gospel to proclaim but should in their life and unity exemplify God's purposes for all humankind. W.A. Visser 't Hooft attempted, with considerable success, to steer discussion away from abstract investigations of the being of the church towards a concentration on the functions of the church in the world. In a seminal article the veteran ecumenical leader J.H. Oldham explored the notion of a free society in which leaders recognized their responsibility to citizens and to God. Christian faith, Oldham argued, can still provide some guidance for the collective decisions of society, resting on Christian convictions about human nature and community. [15]

At Amsterdam the World Council was dominated by the white male theologians and church leaders of the North. Even the development of the notion of the responsible society reflected this in its assumption that the churches should relate to the decision-makers of society and that the ecumenical dialogue was largely among influential people. But priorities and emphases changed rapidly as the voice of the churches of the South was heard more and more loudly and new groups of people, many of whom had been marginalized or excluded — women, the poor, blacks — began to be more evident in ecumenical gatherings. By the time of the 1966 Geneva conference on "Christians in the Technical and Social Revolutions of our Time", the theological pivots had become "rapid social change" and "revolution". The situation to be addressed was now different. The agenda was no longer post-war reconstruction but how to respond faithfully in an explosive situation of exploitation and injustice. The voice of the poor was frequently heard, demanding that the churches address the pressing issues of injustice, racism, apartheid and poverty. Many of the traditional concerns of the ecumenical movement were often dismissed as self-indulgent and inward-looking in a world where hunger, deprivation and oppression should be at the top of the Christian agenda. What has been called an "ethical ecclesiology" was clearly emerging; in some extreme situations, it was said, failure to take a stand on ethical issues impugned the integrity of the church:

> Although in history the guiding hand of God is hidden and can be discerned only through the venture of faith, in some historical situations the humanity of man is so clearly at stake that the church as a body must speak to society on behalf of the oppressed. Churches, groups and individuals who defend violations, thus refusing to see and denounce the sinful attitudes at the base of social sin, set themselves outside the fellowship of Christian witness. [16]

Developing this theme at the Uppsala assembly in 1968 Visser 't Hooft spoke of racism and apartheid as ethical heresies. Those Christians and churches which condone, practise or even theologically justify racism or apartheid are therefore in a state of heresy: they have excluded themselves from the church by their behaviour. The implication is that churches that do such things have ceased to be churches, for certain ethical stances are integral to what it is to be church. Issues such as apartheid, the conviction grew, are not simply matters of ethics but strictly theological issues which go to the heart of the gospel and the nature of the church. It is impossible to witness to the truth of the gospel without denouncing false gospels. Thus in 1968 the joint theological commission of the South African Council of Churches and the South African Catholic Bishops' Conference produced a *Message to the People of South Africa* in which they declared apartheid to be "a false faith, a novel gospel", which inevitably conflicts with the Christian gospel. [17] This was followed by the Lutheran World Federation and the World Alliance of Reformed Churches declaring apartheid to be sinful, and Christians who defend it as putting themselves into a state of heresy. Opposition to apartheid and racism are thus seen as integral to the faith and necessary for the integrity of the church; they are confessional matters, or issues of *status confessionis*.

There has been an increasing tendency to see certain other ethical issues in the same light. For instance, many suggested that the incompatibility between confessing the Christian faith and waging nuclear war, or even pursuing a policy of nuclear deterrence, is such that these also are confessional matters. The WCC's Vancouver assembly in 1983 declared nuclear deterrence to be "contrary to our faith in Jesus Christ who is our life and peace". [18] And Ulrich Duchrow, arguing that the injustices of the world economic system have made it a confessional issue, calls for a confessional response modelled on the Barmen Declaration of 1934, developed in opposition to Hitler:

> Do thieves, profiteers and the victims of their depredations, all of whom call themselves Christians, continue to share together in the eucharist even if the thieves blatantly go on thieving and profiteering and denying or disguising its reality and extent? A Barmen-style theological declaration in a Western industrial society would need to deal explicitly with this guilt and offer encouragement and practical guidance for conversion. [19]

Christian profiteers and exploiters, the suggestion is, need to repent and change their ways or risk exclusion from the church.

At Vancouver this "confessional" approach was brought together with the suggestion that unity should take a conciliar form using the theological concept of covenant, which has also been influential in social thought through the years. The assembly recommended that the churches at all levels "enter into a covenant in a conciliar process":

> — to confess Christ, the life of the world, as the Lord over the idols of our times, the Good Shepherd who "brings life and life in its fullness" for his people and for all creation;

— to resist the demonic powers of death inherent in racism, sexism, class domination, caste oppression and militarism;
— to repudiate the misuse of economic organization, science and technology in the service of powers and principalities and against people.

The assembly called for "a clear covenanting commitment to work for justice and peace" and rejection of "the heretical forces which use the name of Christ or 'Christian' to legitimize the powers of death". [20]

After much difficult negotiation and planning, the Vancouver initiative resulted in a world convocation on "Justice, Peace and the Integrity of Creation", held in Seoul, Korea, in March 1990. The convocation rested on a strong conviction that ecclesiology and ethics belonged together, but there was a good deal of confusion about the nature of the relationship. Delegates had not been mandated by their churches to enter into a covenant, and the agenda expanded so fast that things got out of hand. Thus, the outcome did little to clarify the situation or the theological or ethical issues. The ecclesiological and theological implications of the Seoul gathering have never been adequately examined, but the convocation did, after a certain amount of confusion, produce a series of ten affirmations. Each included a confessional statement and practical commitments to resist negative forces and support all positive endeavours. The affirmations declared that all exercise of power is accountable to God, supported the preferential option for the poor, the equal value of all races and peoples, the community of women and men, the need to found community upon truth, the peace of the Lord Jesus Christ, the creation as beloved of God and the earth as the Lord's, the dignity and commitment of the younger generation, and human rights as given by God. [21]

The Seoul convocation has been roundly attacked for sweeping idealist judgments, for lack of careful preparation, for a fairly naive idealism and for oversimplifying complex issues. US Lutheran theologian George Lindbeck, for example, declared the JPIC programmes to be "more than questionable to the extent they become the goal and motive rather than fruit and by-product of Christian life together" and concluded that JPIC involved replacing justification by faith with justification by service.[22] But the whole pressure of recent ecumenical thought has been towards seeing ethical action in a liberationist or Barthian way as far more than a by-product or fruit of faith. Ronald Preston, an outspoken "friendly critic" who was himself deeply involved at an earlier stage in ecumenical social ethics, has suggested that Seoul showed that the WCC no longer has a consistent, carefully thought-through and incremental social teaching, which could be compared with the social teaching of the Roman Catholic Church, or which is capable of entering into dialogue with contemporary social theory.[23] In this he is probably right. The WCC's understanding of how to do social ethics has certainly changed. Much of its constituency today rejects, for better or for worse, the need for and usefulness of magisterial teaching from on high.

But the WCC today does have a capacity which it did not have in the past to speak for the *silenced*, to express the anger, outrage and expectation of the victims of oppression and exploitation. It may not be very good at developing a social theology which can critically articulate these cries. But that may come. Meanwhile it is important to recognize that the Christian church is one of the few bodies which is capable of speaking for the silenced and indeed has a positive mandate to do so. This voice, even if disjointed, angry and simplistic, must surely be a major ingredient in any serious Christian involvement with social issues today. And although the Justice, Peace and the Integrity of Creation process appears to have had little impact on the intellectual, political or economic power centres, and has not in fact involved the churches as institutions in any significant degree of binding "covenants", there is evidence that it has had, and continues to have, considerable influence at the grassroots in various parts of the world. And if the church essentially is people, what happens in the grassroots is of profound importance.

Out of these uncertainties and convictions the ecclesiology and ethics studies that lie behind this book arose, attempting to clarify the relation between the being of the church and its stance on the issues of the day, between the confession of the faith and the life-style that is proper for Christians.

NOTES

[1] K.S. Latourette, in Ruth Rouse and Stephen Neill, eds, *A History of the Ecumenical Movement, 1517-1948*, 2nd ed, London, SPCK, 1967, p.362.

[2] Norman Goodall, *The Ecumenical Movement*, Oxford, Oxford UP, 1961, p.23.

[3] *Ibid.*, p.30.

[4] Kenneth Grubb, ed., *The Church and the State*, London, Oxford UP, 1939.

[5] Cited in Goodall, *op. cit.*, pp.38f.

[6] Cited by Goodall, *ibid.*, pp.60f.

[7] *The Churches Survey Their Task: The Report of the Conference at Oxford, July 1937, on Church, Community and State*, London, Allen & Unwin, 1938, p.10.

[8] In W.A. Visser 't Hooft and J.H. Oldham, *The Church and its Function in Society*, London, Allen & Unwin, 1937, p.97.

[9] *Ibid.*, pp.99f.

[10] *Ibid.*, pp.161f.

[11] Cited by Lukas Vischer, ed., *A Documentary History of the Faith and Order Movement, 1927-1963*, Geneva, WCC, 1963, p.30.

[12] *Baptism, Eucharist and Ministry*, Faith and Order Paper no. 111, Geneva, WCC, 1982, Baptism, para. 10.

[13] *Church and World: The Unity of the Church and the Renewal of Human Community*, Faith and Order Paper no. 151, Geneva, WCC, 1990.

[14] *The Uppsala Report 1968*, Geneva, WCC, 1968, pp.17f.

[15] *The Church and the Disorder of Society*, London, SCM, 1948, pp.120-54.

[16] *Christians in the Technical and Social Revolutions of Our Time*, Geneva, WCC, 1966, p.204. See Peter Lodberg, "The History of Ecumenical Work on Ecclesiology and Ethics", *The Ecumenical Review*, vol. 47, no. 2, 1995, p.134.

[17] Cf. John de Gruchy and Charles Villa-Vicencio, eds, *Apartheid Is a Heresy*, Cape Town, D. Philip, 1983, p.155.

[18] David Gill, ed., *Gathered for Life*, Geneva, WCC, 1983, p.44.

[19] Ulrich Duchrow, *Global Economy: A Confessional Issue for the Churches?*, Geneva, WCC, 1987, p.111.

[20] Gill, *op. cit.*, p.89.

[21] See *Now Is The Time: The Final Document and Other Texts from the World Convocation on Justice, Peace and the Integrity of Creation, Seoul, Republic of Korea, 5-12 March 1990*, Geneva, WCC, 1990.

[22] George A. Lindbeck, "Tilting in the Ecumenical Wars", *Lutheran Forum*, vol. 26, no. 4, 1992, p.23.

[23] Ronald Preston, *Confusions in Christian Social Ethics: Problems for Geneva and Rome*, London, SCM, 1994, esp. pp.83-87.

4. Worship, Ethics and Unity

Worship is the central and defining activity of the people of God. It is something we *do* rather than observe or listen to or talk about. In worship the church manifests itself most clearly, and in worship Christians are nourished for the broader "divine service" or "liturgy after the liturgy" in the life of the world. In worship we are involved in the life of heaven, we experience in a fragmentary way the life that is to come and we glimpse God's purposes for everyone and for the whole of creation. Worship expresses and creates community, *koinonia* and in worship we find an ethic, a lifestyle, embodied and sustained. We discover in authentic Christian worship a deeper experience of the unity, harmony and reconciliation that God has in store for God's people. In worship the search for the fuller institutional actualization of unity is actively fostered, and worshippers are invited and encouraged to involve themselves in struggles for peace and justice and liberation. [1]

Worship is a kind of template of the Christian life. The worship of communities of expectant faith anticipates God's future and challenges the present. Those who sing God's song in a strange land are thereby disturbing the existing order and proclaiming an alternative. As they reappropriate the tradition in celebrating together the love and the justice of God, they discover that opportunities of renewal, transformation and liberation are offered to them.

Worship and the service of God

Orthodox Christians in particular have reminded us all that when we speak of worship we do not mean simply or exclusively set times of worship — the particular and rather odd compartment of life sometimes called the "cult". The wholeness of the Christian life should be rooted in the times set apart; any sharp disjunction between worship and the Christian life is a distortion of both. "Christ did not establish a society for the observance of worship, a 'cultic society'," wrote the Orthodox theologian Alexander Schmemann, "but rather the church as the way of salvation, as the new life of re-created [hu]mankind." [2] Only too often we have made of worship — which should sanctify and illumine the whole of life, which should be the leaven of the lump and the sign of God's love for the world — a temporary escape from reality and a way of avoiding the ethical task. But in fact worship ought to be a resource for the enrichment and humanization of the life of the world.

Worship should shape and enrich the practice and the ethics of the community of faith, for it is "condensed action that is intended to focus and concentrate meaning so that what is done in this nexus of sacred time and place ripples out onto all prior and subsequent doings, the doings that take place in the 'profane' or outside world, resonating in these ordinary affairs with interpretive possibilities."[3] Christian worship, in other words, is the heart of Christian practice and ethics, which expresses the significance of the whole and sustains and illumines the Christian life. In worship and in action which flows from it we learn how to be Christians; and in the doing we explore the nature and the claim of faith.

None of this is done in isolation. In worship we experience what it is to be "church"; together we encounter God in worship, and this is inseparable from our meeting and responding to our neighbours with their needs. In worship we find that together we are opened to God and to the world that God has made and redeemed in Christ. In worship the unity of the church is displayed in such a way that we know that it is costly unity, the unity that has been won for us by Christ. The church, as the Orthodox theologian Vitaly Borovoy proclaimed at the Vancouver assembly of the World Council of Churches, "is called to be a sign, a pledge and a manifestation of... life in unity".[4] This unity, he went on, is most fully shown in the worshipping church, particularly when that church gathers to celebrate the eucharist.

In a key passage the Methodist theologian Stanley Hauerwas has written:

> The task of the church [is] to pioneer those institutions and practices that the wider society has not learned as forms of justice. (At times it is also possible that the church can learn from society more just ways of forming life.) The church,

therefore, must act as a paradigmatic community in the hope of providing some indication of what the world can be but is not... The church does not have, but rather is a social ethic. That is, she is a social ethic inasmuch as she functions as a criteriological institution — that is, an institution that has learned to embody the form of truth that is charity as revealed in the person and work of Christ.[5]

But *how* is the church a social ethic, how does it "pioneer new institutions and practices", how does it function as "a paradigmatic community"? Orthodox theologian Vigen Guroian responds to this question in terms with which Hauerwas would have no difficulty: "For Orthodoxy the answer is that this social ethic originates in baptism and is continued in all of the church's liturgical and sacramental acts".[6] Christian ethics which is not rooted in and nourished by worship is in constant danger of being diluted into something very different. "Christian ethics", writes Guroian, "is possible because a new people has come into existence by baptism and chrismation, is reconstituted and nourished in eucharistic celebration, is diversified and deepened in agapeic union by the sacraments of baptism and orders, and is reconciled and healed through penance and anointing."[7]

Similarly, from the Reformed side, Karl Barth saw the theologian primarily as one who holds an office in the church rather than as an academic. Christian theology must be done in the context of the church, as a critical service to the church and its witness in the world to the truth of God. The same is true of Christian ethics: Barth and his followers deny that you can have a free-floating Christian ethics, as it were. Christian ethics is "koinonia ethics", in Paul Lehmann's phrase. It is necessarily *church* ethics, tied to the life of the community of faith, serving that community and articulating the insights which that community has received and witnesses to as "public truth". This "church ethics" is closely related to worship. When Barth published his Gifford Lectures,[8] some English-speaking readers were surprised to discover, in a book which they assumed to be about the relation between theology and ethics, substantial discussions of the service of God in worship *(Gottesdienst)* alongside long treatments of the political worship or service of God and the state as the servant of God. Barth was suggesting, in this book as elsewhere, that worship, including necessarily the preaching of the word, is a central dimension of the broader service of God in responding to the needs of the world and confronting the principalities and powers that hold sway there.[9]

A caveat has to be entered here. A church that tries to be the church in an enclosed way, washing its hands of "the world" and its concerns, unwilling to be challenged and enriched by what happens beyond its bounds, turned in on itself *(incurvatus in se)* in its life and worship and not open to the world and to the coming reign of God — such a church is in a thoroughly problematic position. A church that forgets its mission or assimilates itself into the power structures of society is neither making nor exemplifying a lively Christian ethic. The social ethic which churches in some contexts present is in fact more a reflection and reinforcement of the alignments, divisions, hostilities and suspicions of the societies in which they exist. And a ghetto existence, isolated from others by a belief system and life-style which make no claim to broader relevance, like the Amish people in Pennsylvania, is not really an option for Christian churches striving to be faithful in pointing to God's reign. Hauerwas is correct in affirming that "the first social ethical task of the church is to be the church — the servant community... The church does not have a social ethic; the church is a social ethic." But his preface to this quotation is more questionable: "I am in fact challenging the very idea that Christian social ethics is primarily an attempt to make the world more peaceable or just."[10] Because the life and worship of the church are oriented to the reign of God they inevitably have a bearing on the life of the world.

The ambiguity of worship

Such a relationship between worship, the central, sustaining activity of the household of faith, and ethics has not gone unchallenged. For Jose Miranda, the Old Testament prophets are seen as uniformly opposed to the cult because "to know Jahweh is to do justice and compassion and right to the needy", whereas worship has become understood as an *alternative* to the service of the neighbour, which is the only path to the true God. The cult, in other words, leads inexorably to idolatry and sinful practice. [11] In a similar vein Jon Sobrino argues that we gain access to Jesus *only* through the praxis of discipleship, which is always in tension with "cultic worship". [12] There is no "direct access to God in cultic worship". This can come only indirectly, through service to human beings, specifically to those who can "represent and embody the total otherness of God in historical terms, namely the poor and oppressed". [13] Interest in worship converts Christianity into a "religion", Sobrino argues, using that term in a pejorative way reminiscent of Karl Barth.

For such liberation theologians worship is not just superfluous, but is a distraction from discipleship, a temptation and a disguise for the doing of injustice. At the same time, some sympathetic critics have expressed surprise that so many liberation theologians are actively and apparently uncritically involved in "ordinary" Christian worship. In so doing, they are accused of having failed to assimilate Marx's criticisms of religion, and thus encouraging behaviour that is archaic, alienating and fundamentally superstitious. According to Alasdair Kee, partly because of liberation theology's continuing and rather traditional affirmation of the importance of the practice of worship, it has failed the very people to whom it is committed. [14] This line of argument cannot be lightly dismissed, particularly by Protestants. There is much to suggest that what is labelled "Christian worship" can indeed obstruct faithful Christian practice and offer a false way to God which bypasses the neighbour and all the ethical issues of justice, peace and the integrity of creation. Theologians like Miranda, Sobrino and Kee who are suspicious of the actual effects of worship are clearly influenced by the assumption that worship and ritual are essentially reinforcements of the existing order of things, and thus inherently conservative and opposed to transformation.

But in recent years there have been some effective challenges to the long prevailing orthodoxy in social science that worship and ritual are in fact no more than ways of confirming the social order and enabling individuals to accept oppression and injustice, most notably perhaps from Victor Turner. [15] Building on the work of Turner and others, the US theologian Tom F. Driver has emphasized the capacity of ritual to liberate and transform. He sees worship as taking place in "liminal" space, "at the edge of, or in the cracks between" the mapped regions of what we like to call "the real world". [16] An alternative world is established there which by its existence challenges "the real world". Ritual, it is true, is concerned with order and with community, but even more with transformation:

> Social order is not an end in itself but is necessary to make possible the benefits of communal love. But even love is not an end in itself unless, allied to justice, it is devoted to freeing individuals and groups from the forces that oppress them. Static love is never enough, and genuine love reaches out to invoke powers and techniques of liberative transformation. [17]

Worship is therefore capable of challenging the temporal order by presenting a higher order that is to come. Christian worship is essentially transformative. The worship of an expectant and faithful church is liberating. Accordingly, it is proper to look in the worship of the church for insights and resources for the moral life, and to expect that if the church is a social ethic this should be most clearly manifest in its worship, service, sacrifice.

And yet the empirical reality continues to be ambiguous. Most totalitarian regimes in this century have prohibited evangelistic and educational activity by the church and tried to control its preaching, while regarding worship taking place within a recognized church building as relatively inoffensive. Some have even suggested that the Nazis, far from worrying about the movement for liturgical renewal, secretly encouraged it on the grounds that it made church people less concerned with the political, economic and social processes around them. [18] Nevertheless, both the Nazi and the communist dictatorships took great pains to develop alternative secular rituals and forms of "worship" — baptism, marriage, confirmation, funerals, etc. — to wean the people away from the church, thereby attesting to the continuing power and influence of worship over behaviour and belief. [19]

Consequently, as we turn now to an exploration of the ethical content and force of two central dimensions of Christian worship — the Lord's supper and baptism — in the light of the ecumenical convergence most strikingly crystallized in *Baptism, Eucharist and Ministry*, we shall seek to do so in a theologically responsible way that is chastened by empirical reality and aware of the powerful political and economic forces at work in the world today.

Baptism

The sacrament of baptism is a celebration of grace, a recognition of God's choice and also a recentring of life, a reorientation, a new beginning. It is a turning to God from idols (1 Thess. 1:9) in order to "lead a life worthy of God, who calls you into his own kingdom and glory" (1 Thess. 2:12). Repentance, conversion, baptism thus give a new identity, a new orientation, a new goal. It is not simply a rite; it is a life lived to God, which finds its fulfilment only at the end, as Jesus' baptism found its fulfilment on the cross. Baptism is entry into a community of forgiven sinners, a fellowship of reconciliation, not a company of moral heroes.

Baptism, Eucharist and Ministry gives considerable attention to the ethical content of baptism:

> Baptism initiates the reality of the new life given in the midst of the present world. It gives participation in the community of the Holy Spirit. It is a sign of the kingdom of God and of the life of the world to come. Through the gifts of faith, hope and love, baptism has a dynamic which embraces the whole of life, extends to all nations, and anticipates the day when every tongue will confess that Jesus Christ is Lord to the glory of God the Father (Baptism, para. 7).

52

"Baptism", writes Vigen Guroian, "is where reflection upon Christian ethics ought to begin."[20] For in baptism we embark upon the life and discipline of discipleship, and are called to be people of a certain character, showing love, generosity and graciousness in our dealings and struggling against the selfishness, pride, violence and arrogance which are endemic in a sinful world. Incorporation into Christ has a powerful ethical component, and in baptism we are assured of support and forgiveness in our ethical struggles. Guroian quotes the words used in the Armenian church during the anointing in the baptismal rite:

Sweet ointment in the name of Jesus Christ is poured upon thee as a seal of incorruptible heavenly gifts.

The eyes:
This seal in the name of Jesus Christ enlighten thine eyes, that thou mayest never sleep unto death.

The ears:
This holy anointing be unto thee for the hearing of divine commandments.

The nostrils:
This seal in the name of Jesus Christ be to thee a sweet smell from life unto life.

The mouth:
This seal in the name of Jesus Christ be to thee a guard for thy mouth and a strong door for thy lips.

The hands:
This seal in the name of Jesus Christ be to thee a cause for good works and for all virtuous deeds and conduct.

The heart:
This seal establish in thee a pure heart and renew within thee an upright spirit.

The back:
This seal in the name of Jesus Christ be to thee a shield of strength thereby to quench all the fiery darts of the Evil One.

The feet:
This divine seal direct thy goings unto life everlasting that thou mayest not be shaken.

Although administered to individuals, baptism is incorporation into Christ and entry into a community. The ethics and the way of life that baptism signifies is therefore from start to finish a communal matter. We are never alone, but are constantly in solidarity with countless others, who encourage, guide and warn. As part of the body we are responsible to and for one another. And in baptism we experience and enter a fuller unity, a more comprehensive and reconciled community, a more total *koinonia*, than the divided churches have yet actualized. The main denominations and confessions today recognize one another's baptism, but often do not accept baptized Christians from other churches as full members or admit them to the Lord's table. This is a painful ecumenical anomaly, but it may also be a step towards the realization of a fuller unity.

The Irish theologian Enda McDonagh reminds us that baptism as incorporation into the dying and rising of Christ is baptism into the *one* church, which is the body of Christ. This is not a purely legal point — that different denominations accept the validity of baptismal initiation into membership — but goes far deeper. In our divisions — or rather, despite our divisions — we all share in Christ. The celebration of a baptism involves not only the congregation, denomination or confession in which it takes place, but all the other Christian communities, as well. Only thus is it capable of signifying credibly the coming unity of all humankind. McDonagh goes on:

> In the more confined world of Northern Ireland, with its overspill in Scotland, England and the Republic of Ireland, this understanding of baptism presents a particular challenge. When asked what the churches could do to help overcome the divisions in Northern Ireland, I sometimes, as a shock tactic, reply: "They should stop baptizing." After the inevitable shock effect I go on to explain how the theological and ecclesiological significance of baptism may be undermined by its social and political significance. Baptism of a new member into the local Church of Ireland or Presbyterian Church or Catholic Church has the same profound theological and ecclesiological signifi-

> cance. It is baptism into the one Christ, the one great church.
> All the churches are called to recognize this... However, at this
> level of history and politics, of peoples' attitudes and divisions,
> the unity in Christ, the surrender to Christ, is obscured, if not
> rendered entirely futile. Baptism into a particular church,
> Protestant or Catholic, expresses integration into a particular
> historical community of Christians with its own cultural and
> political traditions which set it apart from and indeed against
> another community of Christians... To preserve the sacraments
> from such futility should one not stop the practice of baptism?[21]

McDonagh's suggestion arises out of a passion that the
authentic meaning and significance of baptism should shine
forth and an awareness that distortion often enters in. In the
baptismal liturgy of my own church, the parents are enjoined
to "unfold to her the treasure she has received today". We
should all be concerned with the constant unfolding of the
ethical treasure that is given to us in baptism, in eucharist and
in the proclamation of the gospel.

Eucharist

"Like newborn infants, long for the pure, spiritual milk, so
that by it you may *grow* into salvation — you have *tasted that
the Lord is good*" (1 Pet. 2:2-3). The eucharist may be understood as nourishment for moral growth and formation. Like all
worship, this central liturgy has an important function of
edifying, of building up the community and its members.
Individualistic worship, like speaking in tongues without an
interpreter, does not edify and should be discouraged.

The Lord's supper thus has an important formative role
both in relation to the community and the individual. As at
Jesus' table there was an open invitation to overcome deeply
entrenched suspicions, divisions and hostilities, so at the
eucharistic table Jew and Gentile, rich and poor, weak and
strong come together and experience a new and challenging
depth of community. When the poor are despised, the
sacrament is invalid (1 Cor. 11:20). In the eucharistic sharing
the divisions of the world are challenged and a better way is
shown. The eucharist involves a commitment *(sacramentum)*

to sharing with the needy neighbour, for Jesus said, "the bread that I will give for the life of the world is my own flesh" (John 6:51). It is not bread for believers, but bread for the life of the world *(kosmos)*. The reverent use and sharing of the sacramental elements likewise involves a commitment to this as the proper use of the natural environment, and is a necessary component of a eucharistic life-style. In and through the eucharist we are called to be holy people in a world that is being made holy.

The eucharist is also food for a journey and an anticipation of the coming heavenly banquet. We find in the eucharist an authentic but partial expression of the conviviality of the realm of God, the taste of the future, which encourages us to seek the realm of God in hope. The eucharist thus involves a proper kind of "play-acting": we are trying out the roles that will be fully ours in the realm of God, just as young children play "let's pretend" games to get the feel of being mothers or fathers or teachers or soldiers. Examples could be found from many contexts; James Cone puts the point with exemplary vividness in terms of the African American community:

> The eschatological significance of the black community is found in the people believing that the spirit of Jesus is coming to visit them in the worship service each time two or three are gathered in his name, and to bestow upon them a new vision of their future humanity. This eschatological revolution is... a change in the people's identity wherein they are no longer named by the world but named by the Spirit of Jesus... The Holy Spirit's presence with the people is a liberating experience. Black people who have been humiliated and oppressed by the structures of white society six days of the week gather together each Sunday morning in order to experience a new definition of their humanity.
>
> The transition from Saturday to Sunday is not just a chronological change from the seventh to the first day of the week. It is rather a rupture in time... which produces a radical transformation in the people's identity. The janitor becomes the chairperson of the Deacon Board; the maid becomes the president of the Stewardess Board Number 1. Everyone becomes Mr and Mrs, or Brother and Sister. The last becomes first,

making a radical change of self and of one's calling in the society. Every person becomes somebody, and one can see the people's recognition of their new found identity by the way they walk and talk and "carry themselves". They walk with a rhythm of an assurance that they know where they are going, and they talk as if they know the truth about which they speak.

It is this experience of being radically transformed by the power of the Spirit that defines the primary style of black worship. This transformation is found not only in the titles of Deacons, Stewardesses, Trustees and Ushers, but also in the excitement of the entire congregation at worship. To be at the end of time where one has been given a new name requires a passionate response with the felt power of the Spirit in one's heart. [22]

In worship we receive a new identity, we are formed morally. By encountering God we learn how to be disciples. We learn to love by being loved; we learn to forgive by being forgiven; we learn generosity by being treated generously. "At heart," writes Guroian, "Christian ethics should be an invitation to the great banquet." [23] Only when two or three are gathered together in Christ's name and when people come from east and west and north and south to sit at table in the kingdom of God is Christian ethics possible. At that table the stranger is always welcome: "Then the king will say to those at his right hand, Come, you that are blessed by my Father, inherit the kingdom prepared for you from the foundation of the world; for I was hungry and you gave me food, I was thirsty and you gave me something to drink, I was a stranger and you welcomed me" (Matt. 25:34-35). And eating and drinking at the anticipation of that banquet on earth provides more than food and drink: "the kingdom of God is not food and drink but righteousness and peace and joy in the Holy Spirit" (Rom. 14:17).

The key section on the ethical dimension of the eucharist in *Baptism, Eucharist and Ministry* poses a powerful challenge:

It is in the eucharist that the community of God's people is fully manifested... The eucharist embraces all aspects of life... The eucharistic celebration demands reconciliation and sharing among all those regarded as brothers and sisters in the one family of God and is a constant challenge in the search for appropriate relationships in social, economic and political life... All kinds of injustice, racism, separation and lack of freedom are radically challenged when we share in the body and blood of Christ... As participants in the eucharist, therefore, we prove inconsistent if we are not actively participating in this ongoing restoration of the world's situation and the human condition. The eucharist shows us that our behaviour is inconsistent in face of the reconciling presence of God in human history: we are placed under continual judgment by the persistence of unjust relationships of all kinds in our society, the manifold divisions on account of human pride, material interest and power politics and, above all, the obstinacy of unjustifiable confessional oppositions within the body of Christ... The eucharist opens up the vision of the divine rule which has been promised as the final renewal of creation, and is a foretaste of it. Signs of this renewal are present wherever the grace of God is manifest and human beings work for justice, love and peace... Reconciled in the eucharist, the members of the body of Christ are called to be servants of reconciliation among men and women and witnesses of the joy of resurrection (Eucharist, paras 19-24).

The challenge of these words in today's world is perhaps more acute than we sometimes recognize. How, in a deeply divided world, can we celebrate the Lord's supper so that it transforms the situation by challenging and transcending divisions and hostility? Camilo Torres, the Colombian priest who died as a guerrilla, believed that in a society as profoundly unjust and divided as Colombia it was impossible for the eucharist to be properly celebrated. So, he said, "I took off my cassock to be more fully a priest", and gave up celebrating mass. [24] In so doing was he reflecting Paul's warning to the Corinthian Christians that because their celebrations humiliated the poor and confirmed division, "When you come together, it is not really to eat the Lord's supper" (1 Cor. 11:20)? Spanish theologian José M. Castillo declares, "Where there is no justice, there is no eucharist." [25]

According to Gustavo Gutiérrez, "participation in the eucharist... as it is celebrated today appears to many to be an action which, for want of the support of an authentic community, becomes an exercise in make-believe". [26] Even more sharply, Ulrich Duchrow asks whether a church which "is divided among active thieves, passive profiteers and deprived victims", is indeed the body of Christ, capable of celebrating the eucharist. [27] And nearer to my own home, we should ask what is the relation between eucharistic division in Northern Ireland and the deadly social and political divisions there — and whether the brave words of *Baptism, Eucharist and Ministry* have in fact made any contribution whatever to the peace process that is now, thank God, underway, if sometimes falteringly.

We must recognize that the eucharist is not the messianic banquet, but a foretaste. We are not yet in the kingdom for whose coming we pray. The eucharist is nourishment for those *seeking* the kingdom and its justice, not the feast at the end of the journey. Passive acceptance of injustice, hostility and division may well make our eucharists questionable. We need today to recover ways in which the eucharist may be a healing, effective, transforming sign of community and hope, as well as of commitment to overcoming division.

It is significant in this connection that Gutiérrez, besides pointing to the danger of the eucharist becoming an exercise in make-believe, also says: "The first task of the church is to celebrate with joy the gift of the salvific action of God in humanity, accomplished through the death and resurrection of Christ. This is the eucharistic memorial and thanksgiving." [28] Such celebration inevitably takes place in a defective church and a deformed world, full of sin and suffering, and injustice and oppression. But rightly used, the Lord's supper can be a mighty instrument for transforming and renewing both church and world. For here we have an authentic anticipation of God's future, an appetizer for the coming kingdom which nourishes expectation and hope. In this sense the eucharist is an *arrabon* — a real if partial experience of what God has in store for us, which is also the guarantee that it will come. At the table, believers prefigure the future, play out their roles in the kingdom, present an image, a model of the kingdom, and themselves enjoy something here and now of the conviviality of the messianic banquet.

Archbishop Trevor Huddleston once said that the church's concern with the Real Presence of Christ in the eucharist sometimes seems to distract it from the Real Presence of Christ in the neighbour. Another Anglo-Catholic, Frank Weston, the Bishop of Zanzibar, made a similar point in the 1920s:

> You cannot worship Jesus in the tabernacle if you do not pity Jesus in the slum... And it is folly, it is madness, to suppose that you can worship Jesus in the sacrament and Jesus on the throne of glory when you are sweating him in the souls and bodies of his children... Go out and look for Jesus in the ragged, in the naked, and in the oppressed and sweated, in those who have lost hope, in those who are struggling to make good. Look for Jesus. And when you see him, gird yourself with his towel, and try to wash his feet. [29]

In the eucharist we learn to discern Jesus where he is, and find the resources to serve him.

* * *

All Christians should be concerned with the constant unfolding of the ethical treasure that is given to us in baptism, in eucharist and in the proclamation of the gospel. For as Stanley Hauerwas says, baptism and eucharist "are the essential rituals of our politics". They are not simply motives or causes for social witness; "These liturgies are our effective social work. For if the church *is* rather than has a social ethic, these actions are our most important social witness. It is in baptism and the eucharist that we see most clearly the marks of God's kingdom in the world. They set our standard, as we try to bring every aspect of our lives under their sway." [30]

An ethic that strives to be Christian must, I believe, be rooted in the being and activity of a church which has at its

60

heart the unity of word and sacrament — a proclamation of the Christian mystery which is our truest and deepest contribution to the life of the world. In authentic Christian worship believers are nourished to seek God's reign and God's righteousness, and learn to discern the Lord's presence in the hungry, thirsty, naked, sick and imprisoned neighbour. Thus Christian witness and service emerge from the heart of the life of the church; and if they do not, the very integrity of the congregation's faith is impugned. Unless believers are striving to be disciples, witnessing to the truth, loving their neighbours and seeking God's reign and God's justice the significance of the church as a sign and foretaste of the reign of God is called into question.

NOTES

[1] See Thomas F. Best and Dagmar Heller, eds, *So We Believe, So We Pray: Towards Koinonia in Worship*, Geneva, WCC, 1995, pp. xi-xii.

[2] Alexander Schmemann, *Introduction to Liturgical Theology*, Crestwood, NY, St Vladimir's, 1986, p.29.

[3] Wayne A. Meeks, *The Origins of Christian Morality*, New Haven, Yale UP, 1993, p.92.

[4] Vitaly Borovoy, "Life in Unity". Unpublished address, WCC Sixth Assembly, Vancouver, August 1983.

[5] Stanley Hauerwas, *Truthfulness and Tragedy*, Notre Dame, IN, Notre Dame UP, 1977, pp.142f.

[6] Vigen Guroian, *Incarnate Love: Essays in Orthodox Ethics*, Notre Dame, IN, Notre Dame UP, 1989, p.69.

[7] *Ibid.*, p.54.

[8] *The Knowledge of God and the Service of God*, London, Hodder & Stoughton, 1938.

[9] On this see particularly Bernd Wannenwetsch, "The Political Worship of the Church: A Critical and Empowering Practice", *Modern Theology*, vol. 12, no. 3, 1996, pp.269-99.

[10] Stanley Hauerwas, *The Peaceable Kingdom*, London, SCM, 1984, p. 99.

[11] Jose Miranda, *Marx and the Bible*, London, SCM, 1977, pp.53ff.

[12] Jon Sobrino, *Christology at the Crossroads*, London, SCM, 1978, p.275. "I would help the Salvadoreans to replace their popular 'superstitious' religiosity with a more sophisticated kind," he wrote of his initial intentions on going from Europe as a missionary to El Salvador; *The Christian Century*, 3 April 1991.

[13] *Christology at the Crossroad*, p.277.

[14] Alasdair Kee, *Marx and the Failure of Liberation Theology*, London, SCM, 1990.

[15] Victor Turner, *The Ritual Process: Structure and Anti-Structure*, Harmondsworth, UK, Penguin, 1969.

[16] Tom F. Driver, *The Magic of Ritual*, New York, HarperCollins, 1991, p.80.

[17] *Ibid.*, p.132.

[18] For the relevant citations, see Dermot A. Lane, *Foundations for a Social Theology*, Dublin, Gill & Macmillan, 1984, pp.143f., 182.

[19] See Christel Lane, *The Rites of Rulers: Ritual in Industrial Society — The Soviet Case*, Cambridge, Cambridge UP, 1981.

[20] Guroian, *op. cit.*, p.56.

[21] Enda McDonagh, *Between Chaos and New Creation*, Dublin, Gill & Macmillan, 1986, pp.84f.

[22] Cited in D. Forrester, J.I.H. McDonald and Gian Tellini, *Encounter with God: An Introduction to Christian Worship and Practice*, Edinburgh, T. & T. Clark, 2d ed., 1996, p.198.

[23] Guroian, *op. cit.*, p.70.

[24] Cited in J. Gerassi, ed., *Camilo Torres: Revolutionary Priest*, Harmondsworth, UK, Penguin, 1979, p.9.

[25] Cited in G. Wainwright, *Doxology*, London, Epworth, 1980, pp.402,568n987.

[26] G. Gutiérrez, *A Theology of Liberation*, London, SCM, 1974, p.137.

[27] U. Duchrow, *Global Economy*, p.137.

[28] Gutiérrez, *op. cit.*, p.262.

[29] Cited in Kenneth Leech, *The Eye of the Storm: Spiritual Resources for the Pursuit of Justice*, London, Darton, Longman & Todd, 1992, p.149.

[30] S. Hauerwas, *op. cit.*, p.108.

5. Baptism, Eucharist and Ethics: An Indian Case

You can tell a great deal about a people by its arrangements for food and for feeding. These are among the clearest indicators of the understanding of purity and pollution integral to a people's worldview. Rules specifying those with whom one may eat and drink define the social structure and express an understanding of community and of hierarchy. In a traditional Muslim family in India, for instance, the superiority of male over female is shown by the fact that the women prepare and serve the food but eat only after the men have finished. Similarly, in almost all societies, servants eat after their employers, and in a different place. People who eat foods which others regard as unclean are usually themselves treated as participating in the pollution.

Nowhere were food rules more obviously central than in traditional India, where the caste system incorporated understandings of purity and of pollution which found a variety of religious justifications. In traditional Indian society eating, drinking and smoking were moments with a particular danger of pollution — through eating or drinking the wrong foods, or foods that have been prepared by polluted people, or through contact with impure people, or through sharing the meal with people who are ritually and socially impure. What one eats, from whom one receives food, and those with whom one eats all express a person's caste status. Meals are ritualized in a way that has changed very slowly, even in the face of modernity and urbanization. The preparation of food and the purity of those who prepare it and of all the equipment of the kitchen are of the greatest importance. As Mandelbaum puts it:

> Who handles the food while it is being prepared for eating is a matter of high concern, because it is then in a pollution-vulnerable state. How foodstuff is handled while it is raw, dry, unpeeled or unmixed does not much matter. Directly it is taken in hand to be made edible, it becomes imbued with the same degree of pollution as inheres in the cook who touches it... A cook's *jati* purity does not flow through the food to the eater, but whatever pollution he bears can contaminate food. A

Brahmin cook suffers no ritual hurt if the lowest eat of his cooking. [1]

This accounts for the plethora of "Brahmin tea stalls", cafes and hotels in India even today: everyone may eat and drink there without fear of ritual pollution through the food or its preparation. Yet a strict Brahmin would not eat or drink at a Brahmin tea stall, not because of any doubt about the purity of the food, but because of the danger of pollution from other diners of lower status and ritual purity.

Besides threatening one's own purity and social position, eating and drinking with impure or suspect or inferior people is a challenge to the whole social order. Food rules are hardly less important than marriage rules in maintaining the social hierarchy and the established order of things. The breaking of these rules is a direct challenge to a divinely sanctioned cosmic order.

Similar situations have prevailed in many other societies and cultures. In Israel as depicted in the Hebrew scriptures and in observant Jewish communities today, eating and drinking play a central role. The complex listings of pure and impure foods and the regulations about the slaughter of animals and the proper ways of cooking contained in books such as Leviticus define in meticulous detail the boundary between the pure and the impure. But eating performs a positive role as well. The Friday evening meal in the typical Jewish family is a ritualized celebration to welcome the Sabbath, but it also functions as a focal point for strengthening family solidarity. Central among Jewish meals, the Passover defines and reaffirms the identity of the people through the ritual recapitulation of the story of the Exodus. This history, repeatedly repossessed and enacted anew, not only defines the people in terms of the story, but proclaims their destiny and draws a boundary between the people of this story and people who have other stories or, worst of all, who have no story at all. The boundaries between Jew and Gentile were expressed very centrally in food rules which made solidarity and easy social intercourse between Jew and Gentile difficult and suggested to many, rightly or wrongly, that Jews regarded Gentiles as inherently impure and as inferior according to some divine ordering of things which sometimes bore little relation to the actual social order.

It has been strongly argued by numerous New Testament scholars that Jesus directly confronted and broke through the structures of purity and pollution which were deeply entrenched in the Israel of his day, particularly in relation to eating and drinking.[2] Indeed, the amount of attention given to Jesus' eating and drinking in the gospels is quite extraordinary. The point was not simply that Jesus was a lover of food and drink (although he was accused of being a glutton and a winebibber — not at all the received pattern of the holy man!). He seemed to worry little about the purity rules in relation to eating. But what was even more disturbing to traditionalists and shocking to religious folk of the time was that he ate with all sorts of people: with Zacchaeus and with Levi, with Pharisees and with quislings, with prostitutes and other notorious sinners — people every respectable person despised and feared: "Look, a glutton and a drunkard, a friend of tax-collectors and sinners!", they said (Matt. 11:19; cf. Luke 13:29). And Jesus told stories about meals which were just as shocking to those who took seriously the traditional rules of purity and pollution: stories of a banquet to which those invited invented excuses not to come and whose places were taken by people off the streets; of a great feast to welcome back a wayword son to the fury of his respectable older brother; of a coming feast in the kingdom to which multitudes from North and South and East and West would be welcomed without qualifying by belonging to a particular religious community.

When Jesus found himself in the countryside, far from any village, surrounded by multitudes of hungry and confused people who had been taught that they did not matter much — "sheep without a shepherd" he called them — he fed them and taught them because he was moved with compassion for them. Then, at Passover time in Jerusalem, facing the imminence of betrayal, suffering and death, Jesus gathered his disciples to eat a meal together in the upper room. One from this company around the table betrayed him; another denied him; and the rest made themselves scarce when the crisis came. This was the meal he linked forever to his death and resurrection, the death of the true Passover lamb prefigured in the meal the night before, and celebrated in *anamnesis* of that death and resurrection ever since. There are also narratives of meals after the resurrection: the risen Lord meeting with disciples on the Emmaus road and being made known to them in the breaking of bread, the breakfast by the lakeside.

Eating and drinking were thus central aspects of Jesus' life and work, enactments of his message; and the significance of his table fellowship, which broke through the barriers of purity and pollution that stood in the way of inclusive fellowship, can hardly be exaggerated. Norman Perrin has argued for a direct connection between Jesus' pattern of eating and drinking and the calls for his death.[3] Another scholar has called his table fellowship "salvation by association".[4] And it also involved a head-on confrontation with the accepted distinction between the holy and the profane, the pure and the polluted. The strange and complex relation between the meals of Jesus and his death suggests that it is not at all fanciful to see Jesus' meals as a significant part of the work of reconciliation, the breaking down of the dividing wall of hostility, the bringing near of those who were far off, the welcoming of strangers into the commonwealth of Israel by abolishing "the law with its commandments and ordinances, that he might create in himself one new humanity in place of the two, thus making peace, and might reconcile both groups to God in one body through the cross, thus putting to death that hostility through it" (Eph. 2:14-15).

If salvation was reflected and expressed in the table fellowship of Jesus, in which ancient enmities and fears were overcome, the same should be true of the prolongation of that table fellowship in the life of the church. But from very early times there was vigorous dispute about whether the table fellowship of Christians need be as inclusive as that of their Lord. The apostle Peter himself clearly had persistent inhibitions about cutting free from the traditional regulations about eating and social relations with Gentiles. Peter's vision on the housetop in Joppa (Acts 10), where he resisted the voice calling on him to eat until he was told, "What God has made clean, you must not call profane", is presented as the opening of the way to incorporating the Gentiles into the church and the inauguration of the Gentile mission. But all the evidence suggests that the controversy waxed long and furious, leading to a direct confrontation between Peter and Paul in Antioch and a decree by an apostolic council in Jerusalem to which the matter was finally referred (Gal. 2:11-21; Acts 15). The principle that converted Gentiles need not take on the Jewish rules of purity which powerfully inhibited eating and drinking together was established only gradually and with great difficulty. But the importance of the issue was vast. Max Weber wrote of the "shattering of the ritual barriers against commensalism" as something that meant "a destruction of the voluntary ghetto" and "the origin of Christian 'freedom', which Paul celebrated triumphantly again and again; for this freedom meant the universalism of Paul's mission, which cut across nations and status groups". It also decisively influenced the shaping of Christian societies, by the establishment of eucharistic committees which were in principle open. [5]

But for Paul the importance of the principle had little to do with the shaping of societies and cultures. It was rather a necessary expression of the heart of the gospel and essential for the integrity of the church. To say that Paul won this controversy, that his victory enabled the incorporation of Gentiles into the church, and that eucharistic table fellowship decisively shaped not only the church but also societies in which Christianity was a dominant influence is the beginning, not the end, of a complex and continuing controversy in the Christian church. Paul could be as savage about other divisions at the Lord's table as about the paradigmatic separation between Jews and Gentiles. In 1 Corinthians 11, Paul denounces rich Christians for guzzling at the eucharistic meal while their poor brothers and sisters had nothing to eat, thus showing contempt for the church of God and humiliating those who had nothing. As a result, he said, it was not the Lord's supper that they were eating. Division within the body had made the meal a parody of what it ought to be. [6]

Controversies about fellowship at the eucharistic table have wracked the church to this day. Many churches (like my own) "fenced the tables" in order to exclude from the communion public offenders and people of bad repute — precisely the kind of people Jesus welcomed to his table! And intercommunion between all Christian denominations is still a distant goal. Jesus' table fellowship has not led to eucharistic fellowship among Christians, although some progress has been made, particularly through a deeper shared understanding of the eucharist in documents such as *Baptism, Eucharist and Ministry*.

Indeed, social divisions have sometimes created and reinforced barriers to intercommunion. It was reluctance to share the communion with those of another race that led to the division of the Dutch Reformed Church in South Africa into a white, a black and a "coloured" church. Perennial problems have arisen in various contexts about whether those of high status might receive communion separately from, or before, those of lower status. Could slaves receive communion with their masters? Did not the communion of the Lord's table highlight a discrepancy between their status as slaves and masters and their status as equals in the sight of God? Can those of different castes receive the eucharist together?

In the context of the Indian caste system, the status of the clergyman who dispenses communion was of vital importance to many. For many years few Christians of low-caste origins were ordained and those who were often were not accepted by Christians of high-caste origins, particularly as ministers of the eucharist. When it was proposed in 1739 to ordain one catechist of low-caste origins in South India, some of the Anglican and Lutheran missionaries protested: "Rajanaiken is very useful and successful as a catechist... But we should greatly hesitate to have the Lord's supper administered by him, lest it should diminish the respect of the Christians of the higher castes for the sacrament itself."[7] The sacramental elements, in their view, would be polluted by the hands of a low-caste person, however valid his ordination. Similarly, arrangements were often made for Christians of pure and impure caste origins to be segregated in church. In one case walls were erected so that the priest could go to the altar in a kind of tunnel, and neither group could see the other even when receiving communion at the altar rails!

The eucharist was thus a trigger for controversies which involved the meeting of very different understandings not just of social order and customary behaviour, but of human beings and social ethics. It was as if the eucharist expressed a view of human equality and of the proper relationships between people which came into sharp conflict with hierarchical social structures, and in particular with the idea that some people by virtue of their birth were profane while others were inherently pure. A critique of the system of purity and pollution which lay at the heart of the caste system crystallized around the eucharist, which carried within itself as it were a social ethic sharply at variance with that of caste.

At the outset, missionaries to India from all denominations tended to be reluctant to confront the caste system directly, seeing their task either as one of gradual transformation from within the culture (characteristic of Roman Catholic and Lutheran missionaries) or as the conversion of individual souls without reference to their social and cultural context. But they all discovered quickly that caste was a major source of dissension within the church, an obstacle to conversion and an encouragement to attitudes and practices which they considered thoroughly immoral and un-Christian.

It was Protestant missionaries who took the lead in the 19th century in insisting that converts make a decisive and irrevocable break with caste. The most usual form of expressing this was by taking part, along with the missionaries and a mixed group of other Christians, in a meal prepared by a cook of low-caste origin, commonly and quaintly called a "love feast" (for these meals were frequently the occasions of much dissension, schism and even violence). In Tanjore, for instance, the SPG missionaries insisted in 1855 that everyone in the mission's employ should eat a meal with the missionaries cooked by their servants, who were commonly of "untouchable" status. It was also usual for baptism to be followed by a meal at which the new convert "broke caste". The early converts of the Scottish mission in Madras were recorded as doing this: Viswanathan "willingly broke his caste by sitting down and eating with the missionaries and the converts".[8] S.P. Ramanoojooloo announced in public after his baptism that he had broken caste "by eating with Europeans and by eating those things that they eat".[9] Arjunan, a 17-year-old boy, "of his own accord cheerfully broke his *caste* by eating with the Missionaries and Converts" the evening before his baptism.[10] Baptist converts of the Serampore mission likewise renounced caste by eating with the missionaries.

Everything did not of course go smoothly. There are reports that the first convert to be baptized by Protestant missionaries in western India rushed from the chapel just before he was to receive the bread and wine for the first time, exclaiming, "No, I will not break caste yet!"[11] Many missionaries were gradualists who opposed such tests of the renunciation of caste, preferring rather to allow Christian influences slowly to undermine the caste system. And many Indian Christians found the imposition of such tests intolerable and either reverted to Hinduism or moved their allegiance to another Christian denomination which was more tolerant of caste and less draconian in attacking their scruples.[12] But an increasing number in the Protestant churches saw the public renunciation of caste through dining together as an effective public sign of the convert's seriousness and a safeguard against reversion to Hinduism. Such tactical considerations were not the only issues: the principles expressed in Jesus' table fellowship seemed quite incompatible with the maintenance of caste rules about dining, and to tolerate such practices in the church was believed to be a kind of reintroduction of the distinction between Jews and Gentiles which Paul had so resolutely opposed as incompatible with the gospel.

Controversy over the caste issue in Indian churches continues today in relation to the position of Dalit Christians in church and society. Indian Christians who accepted the missionaries' emphasis on the necessity of eating together as an expression of fellowship, equality and dignity before God gradually raised issues which some of them saw as clear implications of the gospel which was brought to them: ecumenism, rejection of racism and social equality.

An argument frequently deployed, particularly by Scottish missionaries and their converts, was that Christianity alone was capable of overcoming the deep social divisions which inhibited the development of a true "nationhood" in India. The distinguished convert K.M. Banerjea saw caste as weakening character and making proper patriotism impossible by putting narrower loyalties first. Caste, he argued, puts "an end to unity and strength in the nation" by setting caste against caste and fragmenting society. Thus "a people divided and sub-divided like the Hindus can never make head against any power that deserves the name". Accordingly, he concludes,

> If India is destined in the counsels of Providence to look up once more among the nations of the earth, it will only be by unlearning the institution of caste, and by adopting the religion of her present [British] rulers with all its temporal and spiritual blessings. [13]

The Christian religion is commended by Banerjea for having overcome disabling and enervating divisions.

Yet the missionaries, besides opposing caste divisions and emphasizing table fellowship as a sign of overcoming them, had themselves introduced to India a new and hardly less harmful set of divisions: that between Christian denominations which were often ardently opposed to one another and in many cases refused to welcome Christians of other denominations to their altars. Efforts to form "national churches" which strove to overcome imported denominational divisions and consciously cultivated Indian patriotism, like K.M. Banerjea and J.G. Shome's Christo Samaj or Dr Pulney Andy's National Church of Madras, had fairly limited impact. [14] Some of these endeavours at a patriotic and indigenous church understood themselves as rejecting imported denominations but not seeking a unity that was incompatible with caste. Occasionally their leaders might reaffirm the validity of caste observance for Christians or suggest the irrelevance to true faith of social distinctions such as caste. So Brahmabandhav Upadyaya wrote:

> In customs and manners, in observing caste and social distinctions, in eating and drinking, in our life and living we are genuine Hindus; but in our faith we are neither Hindu nor European, nor American, nor Chinese, but all-inclusive. Our faith fills the whole world and is not confined to any country or race, our faith is universal and consequently includes all truths. [15]

For the prominent and independent-minded Indian Christian leader Manilal Parekh, full spiritual fellowship was possible without dining together or breaking caste, and he even went as far as defending the continuance of caste practices in the south Indian churches. [16]

Yet among the more articulate and educated Indian Christians there continued to be a pervasive unease about the contrast between the missionaries' demand for an explicit practical renunciation of the caste-related inhibitions on eating together and their prohibition of intercommunion. There is, I think, little doubt that this was a factor in the movement for church union, in which South India gave the lead. If Christianity was really concerned with overcoming divisions and creating an inclusive community, if the caste system, and in particular its exclusion of vast categories of people from table fellowship, was wrong, then surely the denominational differences among Christians, particularly at the Lord's table, must be overcome if the gospel was to have full effect in India. [17]

Just as many Indian Christians recognized that there was no difference in principle between the refusal of communion between the various churches and the prohibition of table fellowship between Brahmin and Pariah, so they also increasingly recognized that the racism which led many Europeans, including some missionaries, to avoid eating with "natives" was little different from the caste practices they had been taught to scorn. Some missionaries did not allow Indian Christians beyond their verandas. One of those who identified this issue most clearly was C.F. Andrews. "It would be sad", he wrote, "if the church which condemns caste in the Indian Christian were to condone it in the English. Yet... caste was originally nothing but racial exclusiveness." [18] And Indian Christians such as Fakirbhai made a similar point:

> Another thing which greatly surprised me was that if any high caste person accepted the Christian faith the Indian Christians and the missionaries would tell him that he must entirely give up caste discrimination — and they made him do it! Yet nobody told the missionaries to give up their colour discrimination. Everyone assumed that the missionaries belonged to a different caste and so there was no need for them to have relations of intermarriage with Indian Christians. It seemed that there is very little difference between our caste-discrimination and this kind of colour discrimination. [19]

Finally, the missionary insistence on interdining as an irreversible break with caste inevitably raised the general question of social equality, and how far this was an implication of the Christian gospel. Much of the 19th-century debate about caste revolved around the question whether it was in fact a religious institution. Most of those who tended to be tolerant towards caste observance saw it as a "civil" institution having no integral connection with what Alexander Duff called "the gigantic system of idolatry" which is Hinduism. Schwartz of Tanjore argued that this civil institution had then been taken over by the Brahmins who "made it sacred and immutable". When separated from Brahminism, caste recovered its essentially civil nature and, thus purified of idolatrous associations, became an institution just like class in the West.[20] On the other side were those who argued that caste had an essential relation to Hinduism, so that neither could survive without the other. To strike at caste was to strike at Hinduism, and vice versa.

Both parties to this argument, however, shared one assumption: that social class as experienced in Europe was a secular or civil institution which could sit perfectly happily alongside Christian faith and practice. No anomaly was involved if the squire and his poorest farm labourer received communion together in church but were separated by a vast social distance outside, so that eating together at the common table would be regarded as unthinkable.

This assumption that European forms of hierarchy were in no way in tension with the gospel was challenged by a few Indian Christians and missionaries who rightly divined the radical and far-reaching implications of the opposition to caste. "The West", wrote C.F. Andrews, "must not try to pull the mote out of India's eye while the beam remains in its own eye."[21] The church, he argued, could succeed only if it refused to harbour within itself the racial and caste evils from which India was longing to be free.[22] Andrews and like-minded missionaries and Indian Christians believed that the Christian critique of caste was also a critique of class, and of the degradation and division engendered by the great gulf between rich and poor, upper and lower class. They drew attention to the fact that class had frequently been sacralized in the Christian West, as in the famous verse of the hymn celebrating God's created order:

The rich man in his castle,
The poor man at his gate,
God made them, high or lowly,
And order'd their estate.

They also pushed the argument one stage further, suggesting that even a desacralized class, like caste as a "civil order", raises ethical issues for the Christian and could not sit totally at ease with the Christian gospel.

Eating and drinking and the way they are arranged have a very central place in Christian faith and life, as in most other religious systems. The practice and the theology of baptism and eucharist cannot be separated from their ethical content, any more than Christian ethics can retain its authenticity if detached from the Christian community and its practice of worship.

NOTES

[1] D.G.Mandelbaum, *Society in India*, vol. 1, Berkeley, University of California, 1972, p.198.

[2] Cf. Fernando Belo, *A Materialist Reading of the Gospel of Mark*, Maryknoll, Orbis, 1981; see also Michel Clevenot, *Materialist Approaches to the Bible*, Maryknoll, Orbis, 1985.

[3] Norman Perrin, *Rediscovering the Teaching of Jesus*, London, SCM, 1967, pp.102f.

[4] J.I.H. McDonald, *The Resurrection: Narrative and Belief*, London, SPCK, 1989, p.100.

[5] Max Weber, *The Religion of India*, New York, Free Press, 1958, pp.37f.

[6] Cf. Gerd Theissen, *The Social Setting of Pauline Christianity*, Edinburgh, T. & T. Clark, 1982, pp. 145-74. On the significance of meals in the ancient world as a context for eucharistic development see Dennis E. Smith and Hal E. Taussig, *Many Tables: The Eucharist in the New Testament and Liturgy Today*, London, SCM, 1990.

[7] Cited in M.E. Gibbs, *The Anglican Church in India, 1600-1970*, Delhi, ISPCK, 1972, pp.20f.

[8] *Madras Native Herald*, no. 8, 13 April 1844.

[9] *Ibid.*, no. 15, 20 July 1844. Note that the emphasis here is on eating with Europeans, rather than Christians of another caste origin, and eating European food rather than ritually impure food. But the issue was clearly breaking caste and thus declaring one's separation from Hinduism and Hindu society by associating at the table with people reckoned ritually impure and eating foods regarded as impure.

[10] *Ibid.*, no. 15, 31 August 1844.

[11] S.K. Datta, *The Desire of India*, London, CMS, 1908, p.217.

[12] I have discussed some of these controversies in *Caste and Christianity*, London, Curzon, 1980, esp. ch. 2.

[13] K.M. Banerjea, "Hindu Caste", *Calcutta Review*, vol. 15, 1851, p.70.

[14] See Kaj Baago, *Pioneers of Indigenous Christianity*, Bangalore and Madras, CISRS and CLS, 1969.

[15] Cited by Baago, *ibid.*, pp.30,124.

[16] See R.H.S. Boyd, *Manilal C. Parekh and Dhanjubhai Fakirbhai*, Madras, CLS, and Bangalore, UTC, 1974, p.14.

[17] It is surprising that this issue does not feature in Bengt Sundkler's standard *Church of South India: The Movement towards Union, 1900-1947*, London, Lutterworth, 1954, nor does "caste" appear in the index. There are a few oblique references in R.D. Paul, *The First Decade: An Account of the Church of South India*, Madras, CLS, 1958, pp.14ff., but no one to my knowledge has yet made a serious attempt to contextualize the development of the ecumenical movement in India.

[18] C.F. Andrews, *The Renaissance in India*, London, United Council for Missionary Education, 1912, pp.172,181ff.; cf. his *India and Britain: A Moral Challenge*, London, SCM, 1935.

[19] Cited in Boyd, *op. cit.*, p.41.

[20] Cited in P. Percival, *The Land of the Vedas*, London, George Bell, 1854, p.491.

[21] C.F. Andrews, *The True India: A Plea for Understanding*, London, 1939, p.151.

[22] C.F. Andrews, *The Renaissance in India*, pp.188f.

6. Formation, Reformation and Discernment

Ethics is not only about how an individual should handle moral conundrums, or make sensible decisions, or act in particular circumstances, or reason morally. Certainly these things are important, but this understanding of ethics tends to concentrate on artificially isolated individuals who have no family ties, no specific histories, no particular location in time and space or in community, who are not "embedded". Ethics on this understanding is about universal guidelines for action which apply to everyone at all times, and it makes little if any difference if one is a Texan or a Bengali, a modern Scot or an ancient Roman, an ardent evangelical Christian or a Nigerian Muslim. All are subject to the categorical imperative; in all situations the principle is to universalize one's maxim.

But this concentration on the individual actor and on specific moral decisions and social structures suggests an artificial and unreal understanding of the human being. We are not born or reared in isolation; we do not live and act on our own, but receive clues to our behaviour from parents, siblings, friends, neighbours. Our understanding of what is good and right is not commonly the end result of a process of reasoning, but something we receive from others, absorb from our environment, appropriate, criticize and sometimes modify. Most of our actions are not the result of a period of careful, rational weighing of alternatives, but seem to grow naturally out of the kind of people we are.

In some ways the best kind of goodness is that which flows unself-consciously and unreflectingly and uncalculatingly from a good person. Real goodness is spontaneous reaching out to the other. In the story of the sheep and the goats in Matthew 25, it is those who respond naturally and immediately to the needs of their neighbours — without calculation or reflection, without asking about rewards or sanctions, without considering whether perhaps Jesus might identify with the weak and the hungry and the homeless and those in prison — who are invited to enter into the joy of the Lord. Those who are rejected protest that if they had known that the Lord himself was hungry and thirsty and in need they would, of course, have decided to help and serve and love. But it is now too late. They have shown themselves incapable of discerning the Lord where he is and acknowledging his claim in the needs of others.

Furthermore, many modern accounts of moral reasoning tend to treat the act or the dilemma in isolation. But moral choices and moral actions are normally part of a process or development. One act or one decision points to others and arises out of others. Morality has something to do with steadfastness in carrying through a project, consistency in behaviour, with habits, so that we can trust the reliability of a good person.

Such considerations have led many contemporary ethicists to turn back to an older tradition of moral discourse which was more concerned with character, virtue and identity than with specific isolated choices. Here the typical questions that arise are: What sort of behaviour expresses who I am, my sense of identity? How do I understand the virtue that I believe should characterize my life? What kind of behaviour is "in character" for me? What do I believe to be shameful or honourable and good?

Issues of identity, character and virtue lead directly to a recognition that these concepts are socially shaped. We do not choose or fashion afresh for ourselves accounts of virtue, character and identity; we have to draw on resources which we ourselves have not devised as we develop our characters, learn how to seek virtue and refashion our identity. These things arise from communities that are stewards of a tradition, that constantly tell and retell a story, that nurture new generations. We situate ourselves, we decide who we are, we establish guidelines for moral behaviour by reference to the communities to which we belong and to the tradition we have inherited. Any great community of shared faith, such as the Christian church, has at its heart a canonical story which is constantly examined and reinterpreted, and which presents a rich mosaic of models of virtue and vice. Out of this process of retelling, criticism and debate comes a tradition of disciplined reflection on the kinds of behaviour which are praiseworthy or to be deplored. And the community nurtures new generations by inducting them into the story and thus into the community. All communities of shared faith and commitment are concerned with the moral formation of their members. Most are also concerned with re-formation, because human lives are so easily distorted.

When we speak about the church as a moral community we do not mean simply that it is a forum for serious moral discourse — although the church ought to be that, contributing insights from its heritage to public debate and deciding how to witness to the truth of the gospel in the way it organizes its life. The church is also concerned with the moral formation and reformation of believers, so that they may lead lives of virtue: "Let your light shine before others, so they may see your good works and give glory to your Father in heaven" (Matt. 5:16). It must attend to Christian values and how these may be best expressed in acts and in social structures, and to commands and principles which take a concrete form. In many ways most important of all, it must present a moral vision which enables discernment and a distinctive way of seeing. All are necessary if the church is to be a lively moral community, and they should be held in balance.

Formation

During the second world war the chamber of the House of Commons in London was destroyed in the blitz. When the time came for reconstruction, there was a debate whether the traditional shape of the chamber should be changed to the semicircular design common in other countries. In opposing this apparently minor but actually fundamental change, Winston Churchill remarked, "We shape our buildings, and then our buildings shape us." The same is true of community. Our attitudes and our actions deeply affect the shape of our communities; but our communities also deeply shape and form us. This reciprocal relation between the community and the individual was well expressed by Plato, who taught that justice cannot be expressed except as articulated in the just formation of both the city and the individual soul. The two are interdependent. Just individuals are necessary for a just state, and a just state is formed by just individuals.

It is similar with the church and believers or disciples. The church which is holy is a communion of saints, of holy people. Saints are not people who have arrived at some plateau of moral achievement, but people on a journey together, who have learned and are still learning to live by grace. Characteristically, while Christian saints are regarded by others as good people they know themselves to be sinners constantly in need of forgiveness. The community shapes and sustains the individuals in their discipleship, and they in turn are the agents and representatives of the church. The way a church is structured and operates expresses an ethic and is morally formative.

Moral formation is a kind of nurturing in which a particular sense of who we are and what our destiny is, a recognition of the community to which we belong and a pattern of motivation and ethical decision-making develop. Formation within a specific church provides resources for life and action in the world. But different traditions have different ways of looking at the relation between ethics and moral formation on the one hand and the church on the other. For some, a sacramental understanding is essential, and ethical activity is understood as "the liturgy after the liturgy". Others stress the word of God, and see ethics as response to God's concrete command. Still others see ethics in terms of the life of discipleship. These varying and overlapping understandings relate to rather different emphases in the way moral formation is expressed.

Formation as growth

Christian formation has to do with centring and recentring, with conversion, with socializing, with character-building, and with the shaping and enlivening of conscience. But above all it has to do with *growth*, especially with a certain kind of growth — as being conformed to Christ, as ever fuller fellowship with Christ and with

Christ's people. This growth is towards maturity measured by nothing less than "the full stature of Christ" (Eph. 4:13). This passage understands growth as taking place in the building up of the Body of Christ and as having as its goal the attainment of "the unity of the faith and of the knowledge of the Son of God". Only in the context of service in a church which is itself growing and being built up is the growth of disciples towards their ultimate destiny possible. This growth is never complete in this age, but finds its fulfilment in the age to come. It is a lifelong process, initiated in baptism. It is an orientation rather than a set of answers, a journeying rather than an arrival. True growth is often secret. The wheat and the tares grow together and are not always easy to distinguish. In the words of Edwin Muir's "One Foot in Eden",

> Evil and good stand thick around
> In the fields of charity and sin
> Where we shall lead our harvest in.

Formation and deformation co-exist and grow together in individuals, in the church and in the world because of the fallenness of things. Hence, re-formation involving repentance and forgiveness is a constant necessity.

Christian formation paradigmatically starts with the call of God, with repentance, with a change of direction, with the adoption of a new centre for one's life. This turning, repentance, *metanoia*, which is sacramentally signified in baptism, involves embarking on a new journey in a different direction. The Thessalonian Christians who had "turned to God from idols" were told they should now "lead a life worthy of God, who calls you into his own kingdom and glory" (1 Thess. 1:9; 2:12). New Christians, indeed all Christians, should expect to grow together in faith and understanding, and receive nourishment for this through the life of the community: "Like newborn infants, long for the pure spiritual milk, so that by it you may grow towards salvation — if indeed you have tasted that the Lord is good" (1 Pet. 2:2-3).

One New Testament attempt to express an understanding of Christian formation as growth is a splendidly rich mixed metaphor:

> You are... built upon the foundation of the apostles and prophets, with Christ Jesus himself as the cornerstone. In him the whole structure is jointed together and grows into a holy temple in the Lord; in whom you are also being built together spiritually into a dwelling place for God (Eph. 2:19-22).

Here the stress is on the need for foundations and structures in a building which, like a body, grows and incorporates believers and is essentially a dwelling place for God. This growth has as its goal and culmination mature personhood in relation to others, measured, as we have seen, by nothing less than the full stature of Christ (Eph. 4:13). The whole process of growth must be understood in terms of its goal. Its fulfilment is both now and at the end. Paul, writing to the Philippians, is "confident that the one who began a good work among you will bring it to completion by the day of Jesus Christ" (Phil. 1:6). Accordingly, his prayer is that "your love may overflow more and more with knowledge and full insight to help you determine what is best, so that in the day of Christ you may be pure and blameless, having produced the harvest of righteousness that comes through Jesus Christ for the glory and praise of God" (vv.9-11).

For many people fear and punishment are key factors in formation. Significant modern social thinkers and political leaders see fear as the only way to curb human selfishness and enable human beings to live together in community. True, the Bible teaches that the wicked will be punished, but it rarely suggests that fear of punishment is what makes people good. Rather, God's love and grace elicit a responsive love and generosity which are expressed in good works. Except when it degenerates into punitiveness, Christian formation suggests that actions motivated exclusively by fear are worthless. Indeed, the love of God overcomes fear: "There is no fear in love, but perfect love casts out fear" (1 John 4:18). The fear of God is different; it is the proper awe in face of the majesty of the God who loves us and who elicits love from us. There are of course false or disordered loves. The love of money, excessive love of self, even love of family can be distractions or obstacles to the love of God and neighbour.

Christian moral formation is directing people in community, heart and mind and will, towards the good, and enabling them to delight in the good and love the good and do the good, individually and together. That love is more important than fear in moral formation is one of the great contributions of the Christian tradition. Fear and threats will, in a fallen world, remain necessary to restrain evil. But their ability to make people good is highly questionable. Only those who love and delight in the good will hold fast to the good when it conflicts with their self-interest or when they can get away with doing wrong. We need to learn afresh how to love the good today, and how to transmit through formation the capacity to love.[1]

Spheres of formation

We are all formed and influenced deeply, for better or worse, by our family and upbringing. In the family a child receives powerful messages and examples of the kinds of behaviour that are regarded as acceptable and good. Through being nurtured and loved we learn who we are, how to love and how to relate. It is not difficult to understand why so many Christians in this age of moral fragmentation and uncertainty want to assert "family values" and reaffirm the importance of the traditional family, nor why the church has often romanticized "the Holy Family", forgetting that in the gospel accounts there are several indications of tension and misunderstanding between Jesus and his natural family. In a sense Jesus established an alternative family, an eschatological family, in which faith and love might be nurtured in a broader context.

For Christians a second sphere of formation is the congregation. Those of us who have been brought up as Christians can point to crucial moments in family life or in church and Sunday school when we recognized that we were learning important moral lessons. As a little boy I remember very vividly my parents' deep conviction that Nazism and anti-semitism were evil and wrong, a conviction which led us to share our home in 1939 and 1940 with a German Jewish family. But I also remember my parents' refusal to be caught up in anti-German hysteria and their conviction that the war against Hitler was necessary but dreadful — certainly not something to be triumphed in. I was not allowed to run up the Union Jack on D-Day, because people in their thousands were suffering and dying; and from the beginning of the war I was aware that my parents were looking to the time when reconciliation, repentance and forgiveness would become possible. I sensed that these attitudes were related in some deep way to their faith.

My first church memories are of Mina Forgan, my primary teacher, and the wonderful atmosphere of warmth and love with which she was surrounded. But I remember virtually nothing of what I was *taught* in primary Sunday school. I can still remember the sense of security snuggling up to my mother during a worship service and feeling somehow that I and we belonged there and found love there. That, to my mind, is formation. And I have never lost that sense of belonging in the community and possessing the community's story. These things determine the identity I received in family and in church.

In the family and in church children should experience the unconditional love which sets them free in turn to love and serve. The Johannine literature in particular emphasizes that God's free love comes first and enables us to love one another: "In this is love, not that we loved God but that he loved us and sent his Son to be the atoning sacrifice for our sins" (1 John 4:10). This lies close to the heart of the gospel, and is presented in narrative form in the parable of the Prodigal Son. The son offends against every canon of decency and proper family relationships. When he is totally destitute and in despair, he returns to his father's house, expecting to be punished as he deserves and then hired as a menial rather than becoming again a member of the family. But as soon as he sees his son, the father sets aside all dignity and resentment, runs to embrace him and cover his rags, and organizes a banquet in his honour. All the son's offences against family values and the standards of a decent society are overcome by the father's love in its unconditional and lavish generosity.

But only too often it is not this kind of unconditional and liberating love that we experience in family life and in church. We discover that we are expected to *earn* love, to meet certain standards of behaviour if we are to be rewarded with affection. We find ourselves caught in legalistic institutions where love and freedom have been sacrificed to order, where people's fear of freedom has enabled the Grand Inquisitor to banish Christ as the great disturber of the placid, confined order of things. It was this that led the maverick psychiatrist R.D. Laing to declare that families, schools and churches are "the graveyards of our children". And Philip Larkin's crude and bitter words in "This Be the Verse" resonate with many people's experience of deformation and abuse, emotional or physical, in the family:

> They fuck you up, your mum and dad,
> They may not mean to, but they do.
> They fill you with the faults they had
> And add some extra just for you.

The best of orders deteriorate in time, or are abused, and require radical reformation and renewal.

We are also formed, of course, by work, which is, as Karl Marx recognized so forcefully, commonly an alienating experience rather than an expression of creativity and fellowship. What we *do* defines who we *are*. At least in conversation, strangers seek to place us in terms of our daily work. Thus people who are without work often experience social exclusion, a kind of crisis of identity, a sense of worthlessness. It is only too common in modern society to measure people's worth by their success in work and by the size of their bank balance. The parable of the labourers in the marketplace should remind us that true human worth in the eyes of God is not based on achievement but on grace. Nevertheless, we must also recognize how significant the workplace is for our moral formation, for establishing patterns of relationship and behaviour and responsibility which profoundly influence the whole of life.

The two great institutions of modern society — the market and the state — have singularly failed as agencies of moral formation. People schooled in morality by the market or the state have inadequate moral resources for living together in community. The market depends on rational self-interest and acquisitiveness, and needs to be balanced by countervailing values of benevolence, loyalty and altruism if social life is to be tolerable. The state exercises an external coercion of behaviour. States and markets will continue to have their indispensable functions, but for a community to flourish requires a deeper moral formation of the sort that is possible only in intimate fellowships of reciprocal responsibility and accountability. [2]

Ecumenical formation

Mention of family, work and church as spheres of formation reminds us that there is a variety of churchly and worldly spheres of formation in which we are involved. In some situations they may operate more or less in harmony with one another. At other times there can be a sharp division and conflict between churchly and worldly formation, forcing individuals and families to choose and take sides as it were. Tension between various spheres of formation can sometimes encourage healthy growth. For example, most children's first experience of the church is as a local congregation or fellowship. Later comes the discovery that there are other congregations, and that they belong to a denomination or a national church. Then there is the discovery of the *oikoumene*, the world church, and sometimes the recognition that there are differences and even tensions among the various parts of it.

The emergence of the ecumenical movement in the 20th century has brought a powerful process of ecumenical formation. Many who have, as students or in ecumenical conferences or in grassroots ecumenism, experienced a vastly enlarged understanding of what it is to be church have also found their ethical beliefs and practices challenged and enriched from other Christian traditions. However tentatively, they know themselves to belong to a bigger, richer and more variegated church than the denomination or congregation from which they came. Their understanding of the moral life is enlarged and they have a broader sense of accountability. Ecumenical involvement has thus led to ethically significant change. People gain a new sense of Christian identity because they now know that they belong together.

I remember vividly as a boy feeling that the local Episcopal Church — and even more the Roman Catholic Church — were alien, strange and vaguely threatening to decent Presbyterians like me! Later in student days and then in South India I underwent a sometimes quite painful process of re-formation, coming to know other traditions at first hand. At the heart of this process was a new feeling of belonging, a new sense that we were all within the one Body, accountable to one another and responsible for one another, entrusted together with the task of witnessing to the love and justice of God. And this involved a major change in my understanding of Christian identity, and of the nature of the church.

The new ecumenical formation shows itself also in the way churches behave. Symptomatic of this was the service held in St Paul's Cathedral in London after Britain's war with Argentina over the Falklands/Malvinas in 1982. It was a national service, and only a few decades earlier it would have been assumed that it was the exclusive responsibility of the established Church of England. But this time, it was agreed from the beginning that all the major churches should take part. Many people, including Prime Minister Margaret Thatcher, assumed that as a "national service" it would be a celebration of victory in a war regarded as unqualifiedly just.

And the prime minister was furious when the service turned out to be a sober, chastened and penitent marking of an event which was from the outset morally ambiguous and which caused a deal of avoidable suffering. It is now quite clear that the shape and content of the service emerged from careful discussion among church leaders of various traditions, who not only understood themselves to be accountable to one another but also recognized that what was said and done in St Paul's Cathedral would be heard and noted around the world. They knew themselves to be responsible to an *oikoumene* which is real, although it still has a very tentative institutional structure. British church leaders were aware that they were operating in Britain as representatives of *the* church of Jesus Christ, and responsible to the world church.

An earlier illustration comes from my own country, Scotland. In 1929 the two main branches of Scottish Presbyterianism, divided since 1843 largely over the relation of church and state, were reunited. A period of euphoria ensued, and it was generally assumed that the reunited Church of Scotland had the calling "to represent the Christian Faith of the Scottish people" (as its Declaratory Articles put it). But this reunion had a shadow side, related to a form of racial nationalism. Irish immigrants, many of whom had come to Scotland several generations before, and who were mainly Roman Catholic, were seen as an alien implant in a Presbyterian Scotland; indeed, they were often spoken of as an inferior race. The general assembly repeatedly addressed what it saw as "the Irish menace", and petitioned government to stop Irish immigration and deport Irish Roman Catholics who were receiving state relief or had a criminal record. John White, the first moderator of the reunited Church of Scotland, called for a halt to Irish immigration to preserve the racial purity of the Scots. "Today," he declared in 1929, "there is a movement throughout the world towards the rejection of non-native constituents and the crystallization of national life from native elements."[3] Some Scots even spoke of the unity that Hitler forced on the Evangelical Church in Germany as modelled on the Scottish union of 1929.

Events in Germany in the 1930s alerted many Scottish church leaders to the dangers of racism in the church and of a distorted unity which involves collusion with dark nationalist and ethnic forces. Attendance at the Life and Work conference in Oxford in 1937 was a turning point for some key figures in the Church of Scotland for here they heard at first hand the grim story that was unfolding in Germany, and they also experienced in a lively way the reality of a world church that transcends all national and folk churches. A new kind of leader typified by John Baillie (who later became a president of the World Council of Churches) came to the fore and led the Church of Scotland towards a broader understanding of what it is to be the church of Jesus Christ.

It must be said honestly that in many countries today the churches are not doing moral formation very well. Traditional structures and processes of formation have broken down or disintegrated and nothing has taken their place. In some countries the churches have lost living contact with the vast majority of the younger generation. Particularly in the West, most Christian congregations have ceased to be effective communities of moral nurture. There are serious problems about passing on the tradition in the fragmented condition of the post-modern world. And sometimes churches promote a brittle, sad and destructive ethical legalism. People then find a more joyful, loving and open formation outside the church.

Formation as discipline

From the beginning the church has had a discipline for members, a pattern of life considered appropriate for Christians, a belief that Christian faith must be expressed in action and in life-style. So important was this that some churches of the Reformation regarded discipline as one of the marks of the true church, alongside the right administration of the sacraments and the faithful preaching of the word of God. The true church, they declared, must be manifest in the lives of its members; the church should exemplify, not simply talk about, the ethics of the gospel. The fact that structures of discipline often became narrow, rigid and repressive instruments of rigorous social control, rather than guidelines to freedom in fellowship, should not blind us to the need for a structure of discipline in any church.

The root of the term "discipline" is "learning". Through a process of discipline both the individual and the community should learn and grow in faithfulness. Discipline is necessary for disciples, who are together following a person rather than obeying a rule, who are people on a way rather than under a law. Discipline is a personal rather than a mechanical matter; offence does not trigger a machine which exacts a penalty but breaches a relationship which requires healing. Discipline brings people back into fellowship and holds them in fellowship. But discipline is not cheap or easy. Relationships are not repaired or healed without cost. Discipline is the maintenance and restoration of a structure of relationships, allowing people together to grow and develop and learn.

The Greek word for discipline is *paideia* meaning education, socialization, acculturation, the nurturing of children, moral formation, chastisement, culture. *Paideia* aims at the fulfilment of adulthood, maturity, freedom, responsibility, goodness. The classic New Testament treatment of *paideia* is in Hebrews 12, which sets the discussion in the context of a relay race — the race of faith, for which it is essential to undergo the discipline of hard and sometimes painful training if we are to run and win. The runners look to Jesus who himself, "for the sake of the joy that was set before him" (v.2), underwent the *paideia* of the cross, of hostility and of shame. Disciples should see hardships as God's *paideia*, as training for the Christian way of life, as signs that God is treating us as God's children, that God takes responsibility for us and loves us.

God's *paideia* leads to self-discipline, to taking responsibility for ourselves and for our actions. That God cares for us is shown in the fact that he disciplines us; if God left us without discipline it would show that he does not really love us. God disciplines us for our good, unlike earthly parents who often discipline us "at their pleasure". God disciplines us "in order that we may share his holiness" (v.10) and have fellowship with God and with one another. God's *paideia* is encouraging: "Therefore lift your drooping hands and strengthen your weak knees, and make straight paths for your feet" (v.12). And the race in which we run is a relay race. We run and we win in solidarity and fellowship, not in isolation.

Formation as discernment

Seeking to discern, to understand, the signs — that is, the true significance — of the times is in fashion. Everyone claims to do it. In his encyclical *Centesimus Annus* (1993) Pope John Paul II even set aside universalizing natural law reasoning for a moment to seek, with the help of Scripture, to discern the significance of the upheaval in Central and Eastern Europe in 1989. Protestants and Anglicans have traditionally sought analogies between biblical narratives and the events of the day. In the past there was a great confidence that what Hans Frei calls "the Great Code" of the biblical narrative provided the clue by which the shell of the confusing and ambiguous events of the day could be cracked and the inner kernel of their meaning could be discerned, so that one might endeavour to conform practice to this meaning and direction in events. Sometimes this process seems to have provided real illumination and shaped wise and faithful action; at other times it has overridden common sense and led to strange oversimplifications of what is going on. John Knox, the Scottish Reformer, preaching to (or rather at) Mary Queen of Scots, seems to have been a little uncertain as to whether he was addressing Mary or Jezebel or Mary as Jezebel *rediviva*. This helped to give him the courage to denounce spiritual wickedness in high places, and to discern some of the things that were going on and some of Mary's goings-on. But perhaps the analogy between Mary and Jezebel blinded him to much of the particularity of the situation. He discerned correctly that the times were out of joint, but he had as much difficulty as any of us in realizing that in many ways the problems and possibilities of the time were unique, and presented unprecedented challenges. Discernment surely must encompass grappling with the new in the events of the day, for God's love which is constant and totally reliable is also fresh every morning.

For others within the churches discerning the signs of the times involves little recourse to scriptural narratives or to distinctively theological perspectives. For them discernment depends on close and objective analysis of the forces at work in current events, and enlightened, sensitive and tentative projections of present trends into the future, so that behaviour may manifest practical wisdom in its response to events. The capacity for discernment rests, for them, on imagination, insight, experience and judgment — qualities which one hopes are nurtured in the Christian church and through its worship, so that Christianity contributes to discernment by shaping character and intellect rather than by proposing criteria or tools of discernment.

So here too there is an assumption that people of faith should have some capacity to discern the signs of the times and should strive to develop and sharpen this capacity. This is to be done humbly and penitently, because there is nothing more dangerous than a people who believe they have "cracked God's code" and thus self-righteously see judgment for others and the vindication of their own cause writ large throughout the historical process.

The signs of the times discussed in the gospels (see Matt. 12:38-42; 16:1-4; Luke 11:16,29-32; Mark 8:11f.) are manifestations of a new order latent in the disorder of the day, ready to emerge from the womb of the past. The scribes and Pharisees wanted a sign authenticating Jesus and the message of God's rule which he preached. They wanted all doubt removed. Unwilling to take a risk, they sought certainty before deciding how to respond. They wanted a sign proving beyond the shadow of a doubt that the Jesus movement was the manifestation of God's rule before they put anything on the line, before they committed themselves.

Jesus condemns those who seek a sign at the beginning, before they respond to the needs and sufferings of the world, as "an evil and adulterous generation". This generation is on the make, looking after its own interests, putting Number One first, for its affections are free-floating and unattached. It cries out in a childish way for certainty where no certainty is to be had. It calls for a sign. But no sign will be given it except the sign of Jonah. What is this sign? Jonah was one who witnessed to the new order in spite of himself. He tried to avoid the call of God by running away. Finally, he reluctantly and dyspeptically denounced the Ninevites and their ways, then settled down under a bush to witness their deserved destruction which would be, he thought, a clear sign of the vitality of divine justice. But to his chagrin, the Ninevites paid attention to the proclamation of the kingdom. They repented, and Nineveh was spared: a sign of the mercy and the love of God, which infuriated Jonah. Rather like the scribes and Pharisees who asked Jesus for a sign, Jonah was the steward of a true message, but treated it in a mechanical way as if it were a possession, refusing to recognize that the call to repentance is first of all addressed to oneself in one's self-righteousness.

The Ninevites repented and thus embraced the kingdom, having discerned the sign in penitence and hope. Is penitence perhaps the condition for true discernment? Is it perhaps only when we admit our own implication in suspicion, misunderstanding, prejudice, hostility and violence that we become able to discern the signs of the times? Are penitence and humility the path to insight, and arrogance and self-righteousness the way to lies? Hypocrisy and self-centredness — individual or collective — impede discernment. Pride stops us from discerning in events the judgment and the opportunity that God offers ever anew. Humility is the key to discernment. Only in the penitent joy of encountering the God of history do we find that discernment is a gift of grace.

The other side of the sign of Jonah is of course the not very plausible analogy between the strange and incredible history of Jonah in the belly of the sea monster and the no less strange and far more disturbing story of the death and resurrection of Jesus. Here we find the great central sign of the reign of God, given afresh to every generation and reflected again and again in human history, to be discerned whenever life emerges from death, hope from despair, joy from sadness. Although the Queen of the South came seeking wisdom and discerned it from afar, an evil and adulterous generation is too proud and fickle to focus its attention on this sign and to discern the signs of the times in the light of the Jesus-event. Here is the new order growing secretly in the midst of the chaos and violence of the world, a reality which is only to be discerned by faith, not by formula.

The gospel narratives ominously emphasize that the scribes and Pharisees, for all their inherited scriptural wisdom and knowledge of the experience God's people had of the action of God in history, were unable to read the signs of the times. The signs require a different sort of discernment. It is not easy for intellectuals, for people of status and position to discern that the emperor is wearing no clothes, that a new and different order, the reign of God, is breaking in. But sometimes discernment happens. Let me give two modern instances.

During the second world war George Bell, the Anglican bishop of Chichester, made himself immensely unpopular in Britain because he resolutely and publicly denounced the blanket bombing of German cities and opposed the policy of demanding unconditional surrender on moral and strategic grounds. Hardly any public figure, not even William Temple, stood with him. This discernment of Bell's almost certainly explains why he never became Archbishop of Canterbury. Yet after the war the diplomat and military historian Liddell Hart wrote in a letter to the *Daily Telegraph* (15 June 1959):

> The wisdom and foresight of George Bell's wartime speeches in the House of Lords, although they met much disagreement at the time, have now come to be widely recognized — and especially by military historians of the war. Hardly anyone would question now the truth of his repeated warnings about

the folly of the allies' unconditional surrender policy... While the horizon of technical strategy is confined to immediate success in a campaign, grand strategy looks beyond the war to the subsequent state of peace — and thus tends to coincide with morality. *In this way George Bell, standing for the principles of his creed, came to achieve a far clearer grasp of grand strategy than did the statesmen.* The present situation in the West would be better if more attention had been paid to his temporarily unpalatable warnings and guidance.

The second example comes from South Africa. Years before the apartheid regime crumbled so suddenly, long before Nelson Mandela walked a free man from prison to address the vast crowds from the Town Hall balcony in Cape Town, the "Kairos theologians" came together to compose a now-famous document which denounced theologies which compromised the gospel by collusion with a tyrannical state, or by a nervous unwillingness to take ecclesiastical risks, and called for a theology which is prophetic, which discerns the signs of the times, which looks to God's future with confidence and hope and sees even in the midst of suffering, oppression and death the signs of the reign of God, generating a paradoxical hope and an effervescent joy.

How then do we discern the signs of the times? Discernment is certainly not a mechanical process, the application of simple clues or principles or guidelines from scripture or from elsewhere. Intellectuals and theologians and ecclesiastics probably have special difficulties in discernment, because they have so often lost simplicity of vision and have fallen into the grip of systems or ideologies which conceal at least as much as they reveal, so that they are not open to the radically new. To discern we need to recover true simplicity. Discernment means putting the events and choices and responses of today within the frame of eternity, taking the long view, with attitudes and understanding shaped by faith and imbued with hope. Discernment is a fruit of formation. Only in costly unity and costly obedience do we discern in fellowship the demands of discipleship today.

NOTES

[1] The preceding is indebted to Linda Woodhead's fine article, "Learning to Love the Good in Community", in D. Anderson, ed., *This Will Hurt: The Restoration of Virtue and Social Order*, London, Social Affairs Unit, 1995, pp.143-53.

[2] Larry L. Rasmussen, *Moral Fragments and Moral Community*, Minneapolis, Fortress, 1993, p.70.

[3] Cf. Stewart J. Brown, "The Social Ideal of the Church of Scotland during the 1930s", in Andrew R. Morton, ed., *God's Will in a Time of Crisis: A Colloquium Celebrating the 50th Anniversary of the Baillie Commission*, Edinburgh, CTPI, 1994, pp.14-31.

Lord God
whose son was content to die
to bring new life,
have mercy on your church
which will do
anything you ask, anything at all:
except die
and be reborn

Lord Christ forbid us unity
which leaves us where we are
and as we are:
welded into one company
but extracted from the battle:
engaged to be yours
but not found at your side.
Holy Spirit of God —
reach deeper than our inertia and fears:
release us into the freedom of children of God,
and lead us into the unity of love.

Ian Fraser, adapted